MY LIFE WITH LEOPARDS

GRAHAM COOKE'S STORY

FRANSJE VAN RIEL

PENGUIN BOOKS

PENGUIN BOOKS

Published by the Penguin Group
Penguin Books (South Africa) (Pty) Ltd, Block D, Rosebank Office Park, 181 Jan Smuts Avenue, Parktown North Johannesburg 2193, South Africa
Penguin Group (USA) Inc, 375 Hudson Street, New York, New York 10014, USA
Penguin Group (Canada), 90 Eglinton Avenue East, Suite 700, Toronto, Ontario, Canada M4P 2Y3 (a division of Pearson Penguin Canada Inc)
Penguin Books Ltd, 80 Strand, London WC2R 0RL, England
Penguin Ireland, 25 St Stephen's Green, Dublin 2, Ireland (a division of Penguin Books Ltd)
Penguin Group (Australia), 250 Camberwell Road, Camberwell, Victoria 3124, Australia (a division of Pearson Australia Group Pty Ltd)
Penguin Books India Pvt Ltd, 11 Community Centre, Panchsheel Park, New Delhi – 110 017, India
Penguin Group (NZ), 67 Apollo Drive, Rosedale Auckland 0632, New Zealand (a division of Pearson New Zealand Ltd)

Penguin Books (South Africa) (Pty) Ltd, Registered Offices:
Block D, Rosebank Office Park, 181 Jan Smuts Avenue, Parktown North Johannesburg 2193, South Africa

www.penguinbooks.co.za

First published by Penguin Books (South Africa) (Pty) Ltd 2012
Reprinted 2013

ISBN 978-0-14-353029-9

Cover by mrdesign
Printed and bound by Ultra Litho, Johannesburg
Cover photograph by Mark Tennant

This is for them

Nature, whose sweet rains fall on just and unjust alike, will have clefts in the rocks where I may hide, and secret valleys in whose silence I may weep undetected. She will hang the night with stars so that I may walk abroad in the darkness without stumbling, and send the wind over my footprints so that none may track me to my hurt: she will cleanse me in great waters, and with bitter herbs make me whole.

Oscar Wilde

CONTENTS

The camp at Londolozi

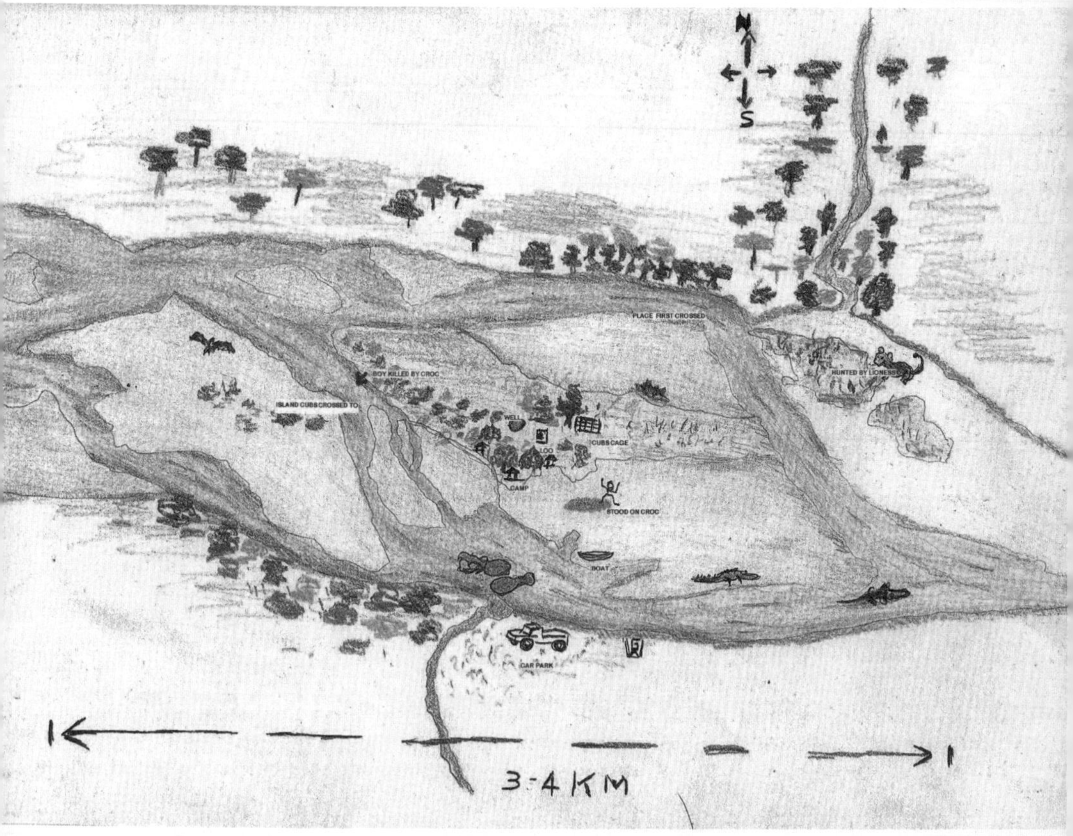

The island and camp in South Luangwa

1
MISGIVINGS AND EXHILARATION

Londolozi Game Reserve
Mpumalanga, South Africa
30 May 1993

Tossing and turning sleeplessly, I listened through the canvas walls of my tent to lions calling less than a kilometre from camp. As they bellowed into the night sky, I recognised the voices of the two Dudley Males as they patrolled the far northern boundary of their territory.

Hhhhhoouuuwww. Hhhoouuuwww. Hhhoouuuwww. Huh. Huh.huh.

The cold night air carried their throaty roars far into the cloudless night across the open bushveld to reach their females who had remained further south with their offspring. Battle-scarred, belligerent and mature in years, the Dudley Males swaggered through the bush with the slow, nonchalant arrogance of those aware of their own power, parting herds of antelope like monarchs striding through a crowd. Reciprocating the calls from deep inside the reserve, five lionesses and their three large, shaggy sub-adult cubs were resting beside the remains of their day-old kill and in no hurry to meet their pride males. The Dudley Pride normally remained in the very heart of their territory while the two brothers plodded to each and every corner of their domain, scent marking and defending their land against the powerful Sparta Pride that kept territory to the north.

The Castleton Lionesses were at the helm of the Sparta Pride; two sisters, big, ruthless females and expert killers who often managed to pull down an adult giraffe between the two of them. The sisters were a living legend amongst the Londolozi rangers and with their five sub-adult sons and three burly daughters they formed a hefty pride that few other lions dared to confront. Now two years old, the formidable cubs had been sired by the Mala Mala males, two robust lions that crossed on to the land from time to time from the neighbouring private reserve. They had delegated parental responsibilities such as hunting and defending their core area to the Castleton Lionesses whose matriarchal rule remained unchallenged by the pride males.

The unusual set-up had its roots in a cruel twist of fate many years before when one of the neighbouring landowners allowed his son to shoot the resident male as a trophy for his eighteenth birthday present. Fierce squabbles exploded among several females from rival prides until one day two nomadic brothers, recently ousted from their own pride, padded into the area to find a fortuitous vacuum. Still lanky, with gangling bodies and scrawny manes, the Dudley Males quickly and instantly demarcated the territory as their own, switching between the Sparta and Dudley prides.

A shiver ran down my spine as I listened to the gruff voices and tapering rumbles growing more distant into the night. Pulling my blankets up to my chin, I imagined the two brothers padding through the darkness, heads swaying slightly, as they moved back to their pride through sandy gullies and thick *Combretum* woodland. I had heard lions calling for as many years as I had been at Londolozi and I admired their brutish strength, phenomenal resilience and even their cold callousness – the characteristics that ensured that they remained at the top of the food chain. But now, for the first time, I also felt a distinct sense of dread. Lions were the big ones, much more so than hyenas or leopards.

In the distance I heard an impala ram snort an alarm, a sneeze-like warning to alert his drifting herd to the presence of the Dudley brothers as they moved across the open plains. The impala were right to be wary; I had witnessed brutal death descending on an unsuspecting animal in a short moment of carelessness.

Closing my eyes, I tried to shut out the image of innocent leopard cubs that had over the years been savagely mauled and left for dead by lions and involuntarily I murmured a silent prayer for the two tiny leopard cubs that were due to arrive in camp tomorrow.

Turning over once more, I felt the anxiety of the past few days creeping back into my mind. John Varty, co-owner of Londolozi and my boss, had secured two six-week-old leopard cubs from a private zoo in Zimbabwe with the intention of using them in a commercial Hollywood movie depicting a fictionalised version of the true-life relationship he had shared with a female leopard that he had been able to follow and film on the reserve for fourteen years. The Mother Leopard, as she became known, allowed John an extraordinary insight into the secretive life of a leopard and, capturing this on film, John indirectly ensured that Londolozi became South Africa's premier destination for unique leopard sightings. When the Mother Leopard disappeared after being mauled either by lions or another leopard at the ripe old age of seventeen, John was determined to pay homage to her through the medium he knew best – the world of film.

The prospect of raising two six-week-old leopard cubs in the middle of the bush was mind-blowing and although it was a dream that I could never have imagined, now that it was just around the corner I also felt some grave misgivings. Was I really capable of becoming a parent to two baby leopards? How would I protect them in a challenging environment where lions, hyenas and other leopards roamed freely and would have little empathy for two small newcomers? Would I know instinctively how to care for them? Where would I even start?

I was under no illusions that what I was about to embark on was a weighty responsibility and I knew I would never forgive myself if anything happened to them while they were in my care. I had gone through my share of personal loss early on in life and I was aware of the pain and heartbreak that lay at the end of the ride. The intention was for the cubs to be released in the wild once they had grown up and this was what I had to prepare them for.

IT SEEMED THAT everything in my life so far had been leading towards this night. My lifelong passion for the bush had begun when I was a young boy during family visits to the Kruger National Park with my parents and my sister Celia. One visit was all it took to get me hooked and that was the start of a long childhood drive to leave the big city and be at one with wild animals in their own pristine environment. Friends and family had warned my parents against taking two toddlers there for a weekend break, predicting that they'd end up with two screaming children in the back seat, but Celia and I were instantly captivated and the only crying we did was when we left the gates to head home to Johannesburg.

I had my first taste of actually living in the bush at the age of nineteen during the second year of my military service in the South African army when I volunteered to go to the Namibian border to work as a chef. I had never been interested in weapons or in fighting wars for anyone. So ducking that side of things by cooking for the army guys who were testing G6 cannons developed by the South African apartheid government seemed a good way to fulfil my compulsory second year of service.

Immediately after making breakfast I'd leave the base camp and disappear on long walks into the bush, observing and trying to identify birds and small animals that scuttled between the clumps of grass beneath my feet. Sleeping in a tent and wearing nothing but a pair of shorts felt incredibly liberating from the complications of city life. It was as if I had come home to the place where I was supposed to be.

Once back in the sprawling crowds of the metropolis after completing my military service, I enrolled at the Pretoria Technikon to study Nature Conservation and Field Management. But after six months of daily traffic jams and road rage I couldn't bear the idea of another three years so, somewhat against my own better judgement, I dropped out and started sending letters to a number of private game reserves, hoping to find a job in the bush. When Londolozi offered me a position as rookie game ranger in the stunning Sabi Sands Private Game Reserve I was over the moon. Finally, I was heading in the right direction.

I was assigned to work with a Shangaan tracker named Carlson Mathebula who shared with me his vast knowledge of all aspects of bush craft, from tracking wild animals and evaluating their spoor to identifying trees and birds. Under his guidance I became alert to the smallest of details: an area of flattened grass that pointed to where a lion had recently rested, a flock of tiny birds calling an alarm to the presence of a snake slithering through the undergrowth, or the screeching calls of baboons and vervet monkeys protesting at a predatory creature nearby – a leopard perhaps, stealing low over the ground.

Carlson and I worked closely together for a number of years and what I found most impressive of all was his uncanny ability to track lions. He seemed fearless, picking up on and investigating the tiniest of clues, such as finding a single lion's hair left behind on a small bush. He walked ahead of me but I still felt a little anxious being on foot close to a lion, even though I was the one armed with a rifle. But those were special times and

I experienced a heightening of all my senses and felt joyously alive. I could barely believe I was paid just to be there.

AFTER THE PRIVILEGE of Carlson's tutelage I felt pretty confident that I could deal with just about any situation I might stumble on in the bush but the venture I was about to undertake was entirely different. Being the protector of two baby leopards would mean that I was no longer an outsider, a mere observer of the situations and dangers that wild animals face every day. I would now be a part of it, which in itself was hugely exciting. Never in my wildest fantasies had I ever imagined I would be doing something like this, but I wasn't complacent about it. Leopards are dangerous animals, inscrutable and much less predictable than lions or cheetahs. According to some experts, they were not to be trusted beyond the age of six months even if they had been hand-reared. They could turn on you in the blink of an eye.

I shivered as a cloud of freezing cold air blew through the fine mesh netting of the tent's fly screen. Winter had definitely arrived. It was still very dark, perhaps a few hours before dawn. Tomorrow was the last day of May and the few short sweet weeks of autumn were already behind us, bringing sunny and pleasantly warm days with bitterly cold evenings and nights.

I had moved out of my room in the staff quarters of the Londolozi Main Camp a couple of days earlier so that I could acclimatise to my new life in a small unpretentious camp on the banks of the sandy Inyatini riverbed that wound in a large S-shape through the thick *Combretum* bushveld. The donga was a small tributary of the wide dry Xabene riverbed which snaked through the centre of the reserve from the east through tall trees, shrubs and thorny thickets that were an excellent food source for browsers like elephants, kudu, nyala and steenbok.

My camp had been specially set up for the cubs and was unfenced. It was small and intimate, consisting of no more than a small collection of tents, including my large comfortable Meru tent, a bush shower that was open on the side overlooking the riverbed and a long-drop toilet banished to the far side. A large weeping wattle bowed over my tent on the right and a few metres to the left was the enclosure we had constructed for the cubs, a cage measuring about four by four metres. I had lined the inside with soft river sand to cushion the cubs' young paws and padded the outside metal bars and mesh with thick thorn scrub to keep predators at bay and offer some seclusion from prying eyes.

The camp was well concealed from the outside world, blending perfectly with the *Combretum* woodland. Knobthorn, russet and red bushwillow trees, weeping wattles and red spike-thorn towered over the bushland with sprinklings of marula trees and thick entanglements of num-num bush, *Grewia* thickets and river climbing thorn. Then there were the larger trees such as looming leadwoods and rough dark-barked tamboti trees sandwiched along the Inyatini riverbed. The southern bank was open with large sandy areas that sprouted guarri bushes and several grass species; tassel three-awn, carrot seed and thick stands of guinea grass.

No one could see the camp until they followed the road that led straight into it. Early one morning, a few days after I had moved into my tent, a small band of francolins stumbled into the camp from the bush to the north and seemed surprised that it was there. Sometimes a pre-dawn curtain of thick mist enveloped the surrounding bush, pushing a wall of haze all the way to the ground. It was beautiful but also rather eerie. Anything – an elephant or a hyena – could have penetrated that curtain of fog and found themselves in the middle of camp. But to me that just added to its peaceful and natural charm and I felt completely at home.

It was hard to imagine that the Main Camp, with its upmarket conveniences and affluent visitors, was just a few kilometres down the road. Along with the other private reserves in the Sabi Sand, Londolozi offered guests some of the best and most spectacular big game sightings, attracting both local and international clientele to its three exquisite and individually designed signature lodges – Main Camp, Bush Camp and Tree Camp. Luxury accommodation, personal service and fine dining were all part of the Londolozi experience. For me, though, nothing compared with living in the bush, cooking over an open fire and gazing at a roof of stars before spending the night under canvas. I kept the front and back flaps of my tent open with only the fly screen down so that I could listen to the sounds of the bush, whether it was the grunts of the giant eagle owl that had its perch in a leadwood not far from camp or lions calling from across the dry riverbed.

Over the years I had developed the ability to recognise most of the larger big cats in the area individually and could differentiate the features of the various lion prides as well as the territorial leopards. I never tired of scrutinising the faces of these individuals, something that had started when I came across the Mother Leopard for the very first time, on the day I arrived at Londolozi. She was already a mature twelve-year-old but her condition was good and her coat a rich deep gold with dark rosettes. She displayed infinite grace as she made her way down a small road in the heart of the reserve, like a legendary Hollywood actress who still turned every head in the room. When she heard us approaching she paused for a moment and, swivelling her ears, swung her stunningly beautiful body around to face us, staring me straight in the eye for a few hypnotic seconds. Undeterred by our presence, she took several strides towards us until she picked up an interesting scent and the moment was lost. She sniffed at a small patch of grass for a while and then she raised her head to resume her original direction and continued on her way. I fell in love with leopards there and then.

A few months later I fell even more deeply in love. Carlson, who was scanning the bush from the tracker's seat in the Land Rover, signalled to me to slow down while we were driving along the southern section of the reserve with several guests in the back of the open vehicle. As we moved slowly forward through an open area along the Xabene riverbed, he pointed to two tumbling cubs playing on the stump of a fallen tree, their fur mottled and coated with moisture from the early morning dew. The guests were thrilled, suppressing loud exclamations of surprise and excitement as the small cubs, oblivious to the impact they were having, pounced on each other and stalked any new object that caught their attention. I, too, was captivated. Compared to the adult leopards I had seen, these cubs were so small, so innocent, and their fur looked so soft and fluffy.

About two years later, I was driving in the bush by myself on my day off when I saw a big male leopard I called Def padding purposefully through the undergrowth towards a small clearing. He had been born in October 1989, the last of the Mother Leopard's offspring and an only cub who was kept hidden amongst the crevices and thickets while his mother went out hunting. Having grown used to the sound of Land Rovers and the soft murmurs of guests and rangers, the little male soon became extremely habituated to game vehicles and we'd often watch him stumble out of hiding to lie in the cool shade of our Land Rovers.

When I came across him that morning Def was an independent young adult leopard. His body was long and sleek and he had grown muscular and strong but despite the fact that he was a very capable and proficient killer, he still sometimes stopped to brush himself along the sides of our vehicles and rub his huge head and powerful neck on the Land Rover's metal bull bar. Watching him do all these cute cat things never ceased to thrill so, when I saw him moving towards the small clearing, I slowly drove up ahead of him, manoeuvring the vehicle so that I wouldn't block his path, but giving me an excellent opportunity to watch him close up once again. I switched off the ignition and sat back, waiting for him to approach.

Pausing every now and then, alert to the sounds of the bush, Def strode forward, his ears swivelling with irritation at the alarm calls of a flock of tiny birds in a nearby tree. He flicked his tail in disgust a few times at this betrayal of his presence as he proceeded to walk through the undergrowth, finally emerging in the clearing behind me. I remained motionless, waiting for him to come closer. Striding sluggishly along the body of the Land Rover, Def appeared on my side, his head drawing past my bare legs where there was no door. I held my breath as his unfathomable green eyes met mine for the briefest moment and he turned his nose and whiskers towards me. As he continued to walk past I watched the muscles on his thick neck and upper shoulders and, stretching out my arm over the arch of his back, I felt his long, curved tail brush along the palm of my open hand. Casually, he moved out in front of the bonnet and disappeared into the bush several minutes later without so much as a backward glance.

Still sleepless, I turned on to my back as I thought of another leopard, the Tugwaan Female who was Def's sister from a different litter, as well as, perhaps, a different father. Unlike Def, she was a fiery little lady. She was born in April 1984 and had given birth to her first offspring, a male and a female in 1989. In adult life, the Tugwaan Female became famous for charging vehicles when one first came across her in the bush before she settled down and relaxed in the presence of human admirers. The tiny cubs I had seen with Carlson and my guests shortly after my arrival at the reserve were her first litter. Three years later, in August 1992, she produced another litter of two female cubs that had since grown into beautiful young teenage leopards. They were still moving together with their feisty mother in the vicinity of my camp and I couldn't help but wonder how they would react to a man with two little unrelated leopards living in the heart of their territory.

An uncomfortable feeling rose in the pit of my stomach when yet another leopard came to mind; a female, who had given birth to a male and a female cub six weeks before in a captive facility in Zimbabwe. Later today human hands would be relieving her of her cubs without her ever understanding what would become of them. I wished I could somehow let her know that they would be all right and tell her that I'd do anything to protect them, keep them warm and safe and that, in the long term, they would have an opportunity for something she would never know – to be free, to live as wild leopards. Growing weary, I kept seeing kaleidoscopic images of these leopards until eventually I fell into a dreamless sleep.

I WOKE EARLY the next morning to the loud chirring calls of a large flock of guineafowl who were busying themselves with finding food just behind my tent. Still somewhat groggy, I pushed the blankets aside and forced myself to get up. Yawning heavily after too little sleep, I grabbed a pair of shorts, unzipped the fly screen of the tent and stepped outside to make coffee. Leaving the canvas flaps of the tent hanging loose, I walked towards the kitchen tent, pausing briefly next to the thorny walls of the cubs' enclosure. Tonight it would contain two small leopards. I smiled as I shuffled towards the kitchen tent, my boots kicking up a fine train of sand behind me. The cool air brushed against my face, carrying faint traces of the scent of wood smoke and a musty hint of buffalo dung, reminding me of a derelict cattle farm I had once come across in the suburbs of Johannesburg.

To the left of the kitchen the marula tree was beginning to reveal the onset of winter. Its mottled bark seemed paler and autumn-coloured leaves scattered on the ground below the canopy crunched beneath my feet like crisps. I entered the large square army tent that served as my kitchen, retrieved an enamel mug and dug my hand deep into a near-empty carton of rusks. Then, after spooning some powdered milk and sugar into the mug, I went back outside to fill up the kettle at the water cart that was parked just behind the kitchen. Across the clearing, closer to the donga, the fireplace was dull and dormant after last night's blaze, but when I poked the charred remains with my toe a weary puff of smoke curled into the air. I headed down the donga to gather some kindling and, fashioning the brittle twigs and dry leaves in wigwam style over the sooty embers, gently began blowing the fire back to life.

It was a stunning morning. A troop of vervet monkeys were dashing along the branches of a russet bushwillow, screeching like children in a school playground and tumbling over one another at breakneck speed. Paragliding into camp from the nearby trees, a pair of yellow-billed hornbills hopped forward on ungainly legs to join the glossy starling demanding a share of my meagre breakfast as I dunked another rusk into the steaming coffee. I relented and threw them some crumbs before getting up and dragging my heels in camp, trying to keep busy as the morning finally spilled into the early afternoon and I made my way towards the thatch-covered carport, got into the driver's seat and turned the key in the ignition.

'Right then,' I mumbled to myself as the engine came to life. 'Let's go do this.' I reversed the Land Rover out from under the thatch, changed gears and, manoeuvring the vehicle on to the road, I drove out of camp.

A herd of impala and wildebeest were grazing on the grass in a clearing as I rolled down a small hill. Pausing briefly to follow the movement of my vehicle with their dewy eyes until they were satisfied there was no threat, the herds resumed feeding on the nutritious stems. Further north towards the treeline the road grew softer beneath the thick tyres as I approached the main dry river course in the reserve. The Xabene was flanked by tall stands of apple-leaf, leadwood and jackalberry trees that cast their dappled shade over the sand as it curved its way through the bush. Changing into a lower gear, I veered off the road and, driving across the camel-coloured sandy bottom of the dry river, I scrutinised the trees for a flash of spotted fur as the wheels churned laboriously through the soft river soil. About fifty metres down, I climbed out of the riverbed at Strip Road, heading towards the main road where I turned left. Increasing my speed, I turned right at the last corner to emerge at the cusp of a large clearing of short grass where the recently tarred Londolozi private airstrip sweated mirage-like beneath the hot afternoon sun.

Ahead of me a small crowd of people had gathered in anticipation of the incoming airplane, and recognising most of them as fellow staff members, I paused. A windsock blustered forlornly in the whisper of a breeze and I felt my ears buzzing as a strong scent of tar evaporating from the shimmering runway filled my nostrils. Far in the distance, I heard a faint droning that sounded like a bee humming on a lazy summer's afternoon. Still stationary, I searched the cloudless sky and, noticing the pinprick of a tiny metal shape coming closer, I suddenly felt nervous. Like butterflies caught in a glass jar, all my exhilaration and misgivings were fluttering in my stomach. They were here. Taking a deep breath I eased my foot off the brake and pushed the pedal all the way down. The Land Rover lurched forward and, bumping over the uneven soil, I drove forward to meet them.

2
BOYCAT AND POEPFACE

She spat at me, baring her tiny razor-sharp teeth and hissing ferociously before she tumbled back into the green air travel pet carrier to dive behind her slighter bigger brother and hide from view. The little male stood as if frozen, staring at me with baby blue eyes large with fear and confusion before he scrambled around inside the box, also trying to be invisible. When that didn't work, he started hissing and laid his ears flat against the back of his little round head. I was keenly aware of the noise behind me, of people chatting and laughing, and I felt myself growing angry when some of them tried to push their faces against the wire door of the carrier to catch a glimpse of the newly arrived leopard cubs. It must have been absolutely terrifying for them and, moved by their vulnerability, I was irritated by the lack of understanding people were showing them.

'It's okay,' I whispered softly, lowering my eyes so as not to stare at them directly and appear confrontational. 'This won't last long.' I let go of the piece of hessian to cover the carrier door, quite overwhelmed by how I felt instantly protective towards these two babies.

'All right Graham,' John Varty said as he approached me, 'we'll take it from here.' He stretched out his arm to lift the travel box to carry the cubs to his vehicle. 'We will see you at camp.'

He put the carrier into the back of his Land Rover, climbed behind the wheel beside his partner Gillian van Houten and pulled away from the airstrip. John, more familiarly known by everybody as JV, co-owned Londolozi with his brother Dave and, having just flown in from Zimbabwe with the cubs, he wanted to be the one to take them back to my camp. Since he was my boss I couldn't really argue, so I hung around for a bit chatting to Jimmy Marshall, an old friend from guiding days, preferring to let JV and Gillian do their thing without me there as I already knew I'd do things very differently. My intention was to take things very slowly and allow the cubs to acclimatise to their new home without forcing anything on them that would add to their fear and anxiety.

After about twenty minutes I got back into my vehicle and with a million thoughts running through my mind I turned left on to the main road and then right down Strip Road towards the Xabene riverbed in the direction of camp. How small the cubs were! Mere babies. And yet, despite being born in captivity they had that innate sense of wildness. Their fear and uncertainty had moved me beyond words and I certainly couldn't blame them for acting so aggressively. They had just been prised away from the only security they had known in their short lives: their mother. How would I get through to them, make them understand that I was on their side?

I parked the Land Rover in the carport and walked towards my tent, hearing the muffled voices of JV and Gillian as they dealt with the cubs inside the cage. Still reluctant to participate in their hands-on approach and preferring to tackle the new arrivals my own way, I sat down in the shade of the weeping wattle and waited until JV and Gillian had finished and would leave for their own camp. Now that I had seen the cubs and understood how fearful they were after being separated from their mother only the day before, the full realisation of the huge responsibility that rested on everyone's shoulders, especially mine, hit me with full force. Watching JV and Gillian take delivery of my young charges had saddened me a little as I understood that these vulnerable little leopards were first and foremost commodities in a commercial venture. I felt their anxiety and could only imagine how their mother felt at being robbed of her offspring.

Musing about the coming days and weeks and the future of the cubs, I barely noticed that some twenty-five minutes had slipped by. The cage door opened and closed as JV and Gillian emerged looking somewhat exasperated.

'Hi, Graham,' JV said, taking off his cap and wiping his brow. 'You won't get far with them tonight I'm afraid. We pulled them out of the carrier and tried to give them a bottle but not much luck there. I'll come round in a day or two; once they've settled in a bit I might be able to get some early footage.' Gillian gave me one of her serene but distant smiles and, bidding me goodnight, they walked towards their Land Rover.

I was relieved to hear the vehicle drive away from camp and, glad to be alone, I busied myself with a few domestic chores to allow the cubs a bit of time to come to terms with their new surroundings. About half an hour later I got up from my small folding chair and quietly walked the few metres to the cage and peered through the dense thorn scrub but I couldn't see either of the cubs. Walking slowly around to the front I opened the door and stepped inside, hoping that seeing just one person would be less intimidating and give the cubs a tiny measure of control. The door squeaked slightly as I closed it and as I turned back I saw a blurred flash of two spotted bodies stumbling deeper inside a cardboard box that had been turned upside down to provide the cubs with a place to hide. I sat down immediately to the left of the door and listened to the smothered noises from within the box, thinking that this was the least intrusive way for them to get used to me.

About ten minutes later a fiery-necked nightjar began to chirr as the early evening faded. Remaining dead quiet, I waited as long minutes ticked by. A cramp shot through my right leg but I was too afraid to move for fear of stressing the little leopards. My bum felt hard and stiff from sitting in the same position and my arm began to itch but I ignored these irritations for another half hour as the night sky darkened and a cloud-like mist of tiny stars and cosmic smudges of gas and dust appeared. That's it for now, I thought, stretching my legs out slowly. I got up and left the cage quietly, feeling two pairs of hostile leopard eyes burning into my back.

I fetched a small black three-legged pot, a spoon and some food from the kitchen and sat down at the fireplace to make a simple supper of instant mash and a tin of curried beans while the giant eagle owl began its deep booming calls from the *Combretum imberbe* east of camp. Way off in the darkness I heard a black-backed jackal crying woefully for its mate and my heart went out to the little leopards. What would they be making of all these unfamiliar sounds without the comfort of their mother? I spooned up the last bit of curried beans and I gazed at the night sky until I started feeling sleepy. Picking up the paraffin lamp from the ground, I pulled the largest logs from the smouldering embers, kicked some sand over the remaining coals and then headed to my tent to unzip the fly screen and set the lamp on the nightstand.

Away from the warm glow of the fire I began to shiver and, snuggling beneath the blankets, I blew out the flame of the lamp and lay on my back with arms folded behind my head, alert for any sounds coming from the cubs. How they must miss their mother; how she must miss them. The thought made me wince. I strained my ears, listening for any sound that would provide a clue as to what the cubs were doing but when, after ten minutes, I still hadn't heard a sound from the cage, I sat up. Was it normal for small cubs to be so quiet? Maybe they had succumbed to stress? Should I go and have a look?

I was almost halfway towards the tent flap when I heard a dull thud, followed by a second and a third. Then the sound of sand being kicked back against the cardboard box. What were they doing? I stood motionless while my eyes searched for clues. Another thud; a stifled sound as if someone had dropped a large bag of rice on the ground. It took me a little while to realise what was going on, but then I smiled. The cubs had come out to play, jumping on and off the box, pouncing on each other and tumbling through the sand. The tension left my muscles and I went back to bed, drifting off to sleep with the sound of two small leopards having fun a few metres away from me. Life surely couldn't be any better than this.

OPENING MY EYES just before dawn the following morning I heard more movements from the cage. I pulled on my shorts, unzipped the tent and stepped into the chilly air. Instantly the sounds ceased and a pregnant hush fell over the enclosure. Okay, I thought, if I were them I'd also be scared. It would take time. Pausing for a second, I decided to go about my usual business first and start the day by making coffee. I needed the cubs to get used to the sounds of my movements around camp and to accept these as normal. Gathering a handful of brittle kindling I lit the fire and positioned the blackened kettle on the iron grid. I rubbed my hands together until they tingled while I watched the pale yellow sunlight filtering through the bush and waited for the water to boil. Then I went back to the kitchen to fetch the last rusks in the box and began sipping the hot brew.

It was still quiet when I opened the lock and stepped inside the cage a short time later. Without so much as glancing in the direction of the box I sat down with my back against the mesh wire and prepared for another long wait. It was about twenty minutes before a tiny scrunched-up little face appeared in the opening of the box. Holding my breath, I remained still, watching the little male shooting nervous glances left and right before he pushed his rotund furry body cautiously forward until he was standing half exposed in the daylight, squinting at the sun. Behind him, as if afraid to be left behind, his smaller sister threw the outside world an even more terrified glance. With the tip of her nose pressed close to his stubby tail, the little female slowly followed her brother, and with baby tummies pressed low to the ground the two cubs took a few paces forward. I remained dead still, following their movements with my eyes as they walked straight towards the thorny cage wall and fidgeted nervously. Then they began to pace up and down, left to right, right to left, sniffing here and there at the shrub, searching for an opening to escape. Every now and then there was a pitiful wail which made me shudder; they were crying for their mother.

I had felt the same sort of pain when I was a small boy and well-meaning family members had taken me to the zoo because they knew I loved wild animals. But instead of being excited, I'd felt the tears brimming when I saw the elephants, lions and hyenas swaying their heads and neurotically pacing up and down behind the bars of their cages with vacant, soulless eyes, as if they knew they weren't supposed to be there. There was one small enclosure covered with a cloth and when I heard it was shielding a small monkey from public view because it had been mercilessly taunted by onlookers I burst into tears. How could anyone be so cruel? I couldn't understand it and felt haunted by these imprisoned animals for weeks afterwards.

The little male suddenly stopped and his wide blue eyes travelled up towards the top of the cage. Stretching out his left paw, he hooked a surprisingly large claw into the wire and swiftly began climbing with the ease of a well-trained soldier tackling a cargo net. His sister immediately grew very anxious. Her features crumpled into an expression of fear and insecurity and she appeared terrified to see him go. She quickly followed him all the way up, only for both cubs to discover that there was nowhere else to go. Clambering back down they continued to pace methodically, almost mechanically. Up and down. Up and down. When they reached the far end of the cage they turned, like swimmers reaching the end of the pool, to pace the same way back. After watching them for a few minutes I thought I was going mad. I slipped down to lie flat on my stomach in a less threatening posture, hoping this would ease their anxiety. It made no difference. Up and down, up and down they paced. How long would this go on? I racked my brain for a solution; something to stop their frenzied behaviour and perhaps even put them just a little bit at ease.

Suddenly I remembered reading about the way female leopards communicate with their young in a variety of sounds and calls, one of which was a soft nasal chuffing sound that had a reassuring effect. I had never seen or heard a leopard chuff, but since I couldn't think of anything else I tried to mimic the sound by gently touching the inside of my lower lip with my front teeth and giving two short puff-like calls. *Pffffffft. Pffffffft.* It had an immediate effect. The little male stopped in his tracks and spun around to stare hard in my direction, his blue eyes searching while growing bright and expectant. In an instant he tottered towards me, barrelling along as fast as his little legs could carry him until he had come to within a few paces of me. Hesitating, he approached more cautiously, step by furtive step, until he was a few centimetres from my face. I literally saw his expression turn from hope and excitement to confusion and disappointment when he realised that I had been the one making the sound, not his mother. Flattening his ears against the back of his head he hissed sharply and then he fled.

I understood their anguish and didn't want to push their limits but the leopards had been in camp for almost twenty-four hours during which time they had had nothing to eat. The combination of malnutrition and extreme stress could be deadly and it was essential to get some nourishment down them, but at this stage that meant forcing the issue, which would raise their anxiety even more. It was a question of choosing between the lesser of two evils so I slowly reached for a plastic baby bottle containing milk formula that I had further enriched with calcium supplements and quietly waited for the little boy cat to come pacing past. In a quick decisive movement I shot my hand forward and, grabbing him firmly by the scruff of his neck, I lifted him on to my lap to offer him the bottle while his back legs rested on my thighs.

'Come on, little man,' I coaxed. 'Look how nice this is.' His body immediately grew limp, acquiescing naturally to the stimulus of being carried in the mouth of his mother, but he kept his jaws tightly clenched as I unsuccessfully attempted to push the rubber teat between his firmly closed lips. Bemoaning my own incompetence, I eventually released my grip and set him back down on the sandy floor. Almost tumbling over his own feet to get as far away from me as possible, the male cub ran to the far side of the cage to join his sister who had followed the events warily and was now staring at me with cold accusing disdain.

Despondent but not defeated, I decided to try her next. When the cubs resumed their pacing a few minutes later, I seized the first opportunity to hold her close to me and to offer her the milky teat. I was taken aback by her response as she tugged at the rubber ferociously with her needle-sharp teeth. Half chewing and half sucking, she tore and ripped the teat so vigorously that the milk poured down her whiskers and chin instead of into her mouth. Frustrated with her own efforts, she lashed out with both front paws with claws unsheathed, boxing the plastic bottle until, equally frustrated, I set her down.

She immediately took off to the comfort of her brother, turning and glaring furiously at me while a heavy beard of milk dripped from her chin. Pulling back her tiny black-rimmed lips she hissed aggressively and I couldn't help thinking that she had the cutest little face I'd ever seen on an animal. With her disproportionately large feet, stubby little body and tiny head and ears she melted my heart completely. What a little Poepface you are, I thought. What a cute little girl. *Poepface* ... I liked it. The name suited her somehow. Sitting back down against the wire fence I took the opportunity to study their different features. Already the cubs revealed a uniquely individual spot pattern above the whisker line which would remain to become their primary identifiable characteristic. My little Poepface had three black spots on the right and two on the left cheek whereas her brother sported two large black spots on both sides.

That night as I lay in bed I reflected on what little progress I felt I'd made with the cubs. The clumsiness with which they reacted to the baby bottle made me wonder whether they might already have been fed meat. I must ask JV for fresh meat when he comes round tomorrow, I thought. That would solve that problem. I smiled as I recalled little Poepface with her face full of milk; she had looked so cute and innocent. And him ... That little boy cat and the way he had responded to my attempts at chuffing had really tugged at my heartstrings. He was so clearly crestfallen to find that his mother had not come back. Poor little boy cat. *Boycat.* The name had a good ring to it. Boycat and Poepface. Yes, that felt right; I would call them that from now on. With their names sorted, as well as the potential food problem, all I had to do now was to break through their fear, win their trust and become part of their little family unit. Snuggling beneath the blankets, I didn't dwell on what an enormous challenge it was.

3
EARLY DAYS

A battered green Land Rover came trundling down the road into camp early the following morning as I was sitting inside the cage with my back against the wall. Expecting JV, I got up to see him, Jimmy Marshall and JV's friend and tracker Elmon Mhlongo walking up from the carport. Clad in characteristic army-green shirt and shorts, leather sandals and legionnaire-style bush hat and carrying his Arriflex Super 16 film camera, JV was full of beans.

'Graham!' he called out jovially as I closed the cage door behind me. 'How are you getting on with the cubs?'

After shaking hands with all three men, I turned back to JV. 'They are fine, but still very stressed,' I said, adding that I hadn't managed to get much nourishment down either cub. 'Perhaps they have already started eating meat.'

JV nodded. 'You may well be right. I'll get Richard to bring up some fresh meat from Main Camp.' He turned on his heels. 'In fact, let me radio camp right away.' Heading back to the carport JV delved into the front of the vehicle to lift the radio out of the case on the dashboard and, pushing the transmission button, began to speak. '964 Main camp, main camp ... come in, over ...' There was a loud crackle between the static. JV pushed the button again and repeated, '964 Main camp, main camp, come in ... over.'

Never a man to wait for things to happen, JV immediately organised some fresh meat to be delivered from the kitchen at Main Camp by one of the drivers at the lodge. I couldn't wait to try them on it. It was impossible to say how much, or rather how little, milk Boycat and Poepface had consumed after another few equally disastrous attempts on my behalf, but I knew it wasn't anywhere near enough to sustain two growing leopards.

'Right, that's settled then,' JV said, clipping the microphone back into its case and reaching into the back of the Land Rover to retrieve two dead glossy starlings. 'Good thing I brought these then. Shot them on the way over.' He turned back to Elmon and handed him the two starlings. 'Okay, guys, let's set up the gear in the donga.'

While the three men went ahead to set up their cameras in the riverbed I went back to the enclosure to fetch the cubs, wondering what they would make of the dead birds. I had never before seen a leopard cub of any age tackle a glossy starling, but was interested to see whether the opportunistic instinct of a leopard presented with easy food would kick in. It was also going to be interesting to take the cubs out of their enclosure and introduce them to the Inyatini riverbed where they could familiarise themselves with the immediate vicinity of camp. It was of paramount importance that the cubs realised that this was their new home, and I had no problem if JV got some early footage of them taking their first tentative steps in their natural environment.

JV had gone into wildlife filmmaking many years before and had produced numerous television documentaries that had been very well received worldwide. 'Running Wild' was his latest undertaking; a full feature movie that would be shot primarily on location at Londolozi, with some scenes in a studio in Los Angeles. JV, Elmon and the cubs were to be the main stars along with well-known Hollywood actors Brooke Shields, Martin Sheen and David Keith. The movie was conceptualised around the story of the Mother Leopard, who JV had filmed for more than a decade before she disappeared at the beginning of July 1991 after being severely mauled. She had been found, seriously injured, in the area between the Mangene and Elmonskraal and vanished shortly thereafter, a mere two weeks after having been seen with her last-born cub Def who, at nineteen months old, had left the company of his mother to become independent. The last traces ever found were her footprints leading down to the Sand River on the northern boundary of the reserve, after which there was no further sign of her. She was never seen again.

JV had been devastated. Keen to use his skills as a cameraman as a tribute to the old leopardess he planned to use original footage he had taken of her over many years. The movie script was a fictitious account of her last offspring; two tiny cubs that had been left among the rocks while their mother lay dying. Enter Boycat and Poepface.

Although I knew it was the best thing to introduce the cubs to the bush around camp, I still felt a little nervous as I stepped inside the enclosure to fetch them. They had only been with me for forty-eight hours. Who was to say they wouldn't make a bolt for it and never be seen again? The thought was too much to bear and I shook my head as if to get rid of it. I sank back down against the thorn-scrub wall with the intention of grabbing the cubs by the folds of their necks as they paced past. Then, carrying the two leopards low over the ground at roughly the same height as their mother would move them from den to den, I pushed the cage door open with my foot and set off towards the donga. Walking down the slope of the embankment through a shady patch created by towering riverine trees, I found a fairly flat section of dry river sand on the far side of the donga close to a wide bend. Still feeling doubtful, I stopped to look around me and then, giving JV, Jimmy and Elmon a nod, I put the cubs down on the ground, released my grip, and took a few steps back.

Boycat and Poepface froze, standing stiffly close to each other and looking apprehensively around them. It was probably the first time in their short lives that they had had some sort of inkling of the natural world; an environment they should've been born into from the beginning. But what was amazing was that something seemed to click inside their inexperienced young minds; a primeval instinct, an ancient recognition that had been passed on through eons of leopard evolution. This was where they were meant to be.

Pressing his tummy close to the soft river sand, Boycat dashed towards a nearby brandybush to seek cover beneath the tangled thicket with his smaller sister following hot on his heels. Now that they were partially concealed, the cubs seemed a bit more confident and quietly surveyed their brand new environment. Assured that no immediate threat lurked nearby, Boycat inquisitively stuck his face out to peer tentatively over the bush before cautiously stepping out into the open. Sniffing at various clumps of grass and ambling slowly forward along the winding donga, the cubs began to investigate, occasionally voicing raspy cries of nervousness as their paws sank heavily into the soft river sand. Initiating the explorations, Boycat took the lead and began padding furtively along the donga with his sister close behind him. Now and again the cubs paused to bat the pads of their feet at small twigs and bushes, to sniff the unfamiliar scents and to listen to every new sound. I saw their excitement mounting as their bodies barely kept up with what their minds were urging them to do.

Poep stared at a nearby stand of tamboti trees, her eyes following its distinctively marked bark all the way to the canopy. Thousands of years of evolutionary data flooded her brain, connecting her almost instantly to that which she had never seen before. For a few timeless moments she just stared. And then her face lit up, like a person unexpectedly meeting an old friend in the most surprising place. Urgently answering their ancient instincts, both cubs trotted eagerly to the base of the tree. Boycat clambered expertly up the bark at an incredible speed, using his claws to help him like a professional mountaineer. He lost his footing once or twice but balanced himself on the branches until he reached the first major fork in the tree trunk about ten feet off the ground. Then, emitting a short frustrated growl, he again steadied himself on the branches and climbed even higher.

Poep too rapidly hauled herself up the tree trunk using her claws for traction, negotiating the thinner branches with the perfect balance of an experienced tightrope walker. She moved far more expertly than her brother and swiftly caught up with him to join him on a large branch where the two tiny leopards sat down to relax. They remained up the tree for about twenty minutes while JV and Jimmy filmed them and Elmon and I watched from the base as their mottled bodies slowly caught the dappled golden light of the early morning sun.

Taking his eye off the viewfinder, JV pointed at the two dead starlings Elmon was holding and, asking him to waggle them to attract the cubs' attention, told him to take a few steps back. 'That's right,' he instructed. 'Now just move a bit further to the left. Yes, that's perfect. Okay, hold on. I'll give you a sign now ...' Bending over his camera and focusing the lens, JV started rolling. 'Okay, now!'

Elmon raised his hand and while JV zoomed in on the cubs, he began jiggling the dead birds around. Instantly noticing the rapid movements Boycat and Poep locked their eyes on the swinging starlings and, emboldened by their tree-climbing victory, they got up and pawed their way back to the fork in the tree, ready to come down.

Boycat was first. Cautiously, he gripped the bark with his claws and, one foot at a time, descended headfirst until the last much steeper section, which proved to be too difficult. He carefully reversed his body and, half groping, half sliding, he jumped the last half metre to the ground.

This was the first of many food lures we would use over the coming months to coax him into doing specific acts for I was soon to discover that, apart from his sister, Boycat had two other passions in life: he had an insatiable appetite and a penchant for water. He'd often sit beneath the tap of the water cart hoping for the slightest trickle or follow me in the hope of catching me fetching some water. Above all, though, fresh meat was his greatest delight. With pieces of fresh meat as a reward, we knew we could count on him to oblige as long as there was a treat in sight. Poepface was never that easily manipulated. Her main concern was to stick close to her brother, the only security blanket she had left in life. Although I didn't realise it at the time, the only reason Poep grudgingly left the tree was because she couldn't bear not to have her brother close by.

Elmon put the starlings on the ground and took a few steps back as the cubs padded slowly over to sniff the corpses. Then, closing their mouths over the birds' throats, Boycat and Poepface carried them off, dragging the limp bodies between their front legs like adult leopards to the shelter of a nearby bush. After a few exploratory sniffs the cubs began plucking at the plumage, shaking their heads and spitting out the feathers so that they could break the skin and get to the meat. Quickly and expertly, they opened the chest and belly cavity and began feeding on the soft flesh inside. I was dumbfounded; I'd no idea that cubs of such a young age were capable of displaying adult behaviour without having been taught by their mother. I felt a huge sense of relief. Meat was definitely on the menu.

Once back at camp we found Richard, one of the Londolozi drivers, relaxing in a sun-bleached camp chair by the fire. Beside him on the ground was a small cooler box which I guessed contained the meat for the cubs. Since the cubs were my first priority, I left JV, Elmon and Jimmy with Richard while I took Boycat and Poep back inside the enclosure. When I returned I found that the three men were preparing to leave and, joining Richard, I took possession of the cooler box which contained pieces of prime impala that one of the guys in the meat room had meticulously chopped into bite-size chunks.

'Ah, brilliant, thanks, Richard,' I smiled. 'And I'm sorry you had to come out of your way earlier than you thought, but if you don't mind waiting a short while I am sure Jackson and Alison will be ready to leave with you.' I turned to take the cooler box to the kitchen tent where I scooped several pieces of meat into two yellow enamel bowls, stored the rest in the gas fridge and went out to present Boycat and his sister with their first serving of impala.

Jackson and Alison came every day to attend to a few domestic duties; another little luxury of living in the bush at Londolozi. Jackson was an elderly Shangaan man of about seventy who in his younger days had been a tracker for the White Hunter and his gun. His eyes were wise and gentle with some milkiness around the edges and his unassuming features were covered in wrinkles, hinting at a life that had been lived with both joy and hardship. He sported a short, distinguished white beard and walked with a slight limp, but his apparent fragility belied a surprising strength for a man his age. Now semi-retired, old Jacks still carried himself with a great sense of pride, protesting vehemently when I stole up behind him to pick the heaviest logs off his shoulder while he was stacking firewood under the overhanging thatch of the carport. He refuted being too old for these burdensome tasks and often grew grumpy with me for challenging his pride, but that never lasted. There were very few things Jackson hadn't experienced during his long years in the bush, but now that the leopard cubs had arrived he was in for something quite new.

Alison was a sweet, kind lady who swept the tents and did the general tidying up, even though I rarely if ever left unwashed plates or stained coffee mugs lying around. Still, she felt responsible for giving the kitchen a scrub before arming herself with the broom and mop from the storage tent to clean the other tents. During the first few days the cubs were usually back inside the cage by the time the staff came in but, since they didn't have a rigid schedule, they sometimes arrived in camp when the cubs were still out with me.

'*Xingwaan anga magnchumu, siya yena loko we wathira,*' I told Jackson, Alison and Richard on the first morning that the cubs came out of the enclosure. 'The leopard cubs won't do anything if you ignore them.' So they paid them no attention and just carried on with their work.

BOYCAT AND POEP stopped calling for their mother after three days. I couldn't help wondering if she too had stopped yearning for her young and I made another silent promise to her that she would not be forgotten. I was pleased that both cubs were feeding well, eating about 200 grams of meat twice a day after I had given them milk formula enriched with supplements in their enamel bowls. After a few further disastrous attempts, I saw that they were more than capable of drinking by themselves and got rid of the baby bottles. When I put the bowls of milk down on the ground inside the cage for the first time Boycat gave a short, insecure hiss and took a few steps back. Then, as I retreated to sit down at a respectable distance, he slowly sniffed his way forward to interpret the scent of the contents. It seemed enticing but he wasn't quite sure what to do. Shuffling slowly forward, I dipped my finger into the milk and tentatively stretched out my hand to gently line his lips with the liquid. Although wary, he didn't move and after tasting the milk with his tongue, he relaxed visibly. Repeating the motion, I moved a little further back again and watched him push his entire head down into the bowl.

Following my movements with cold, suspicious eyes, Poepface eventually gave in to the rumblings of her tummy and slowly advanced forward, every muscle in her body taut with apprehension. Inching her way closer, she took one careful step after the other, all the while shooting wary glances at me. When she had come within a few inches, she focused her eyes on me once more before burying her tiny face in the milk, half lapping, half sucking at the liquid. It seemed that she was finding it quite a bit more difficult than her brother. Afterwards, using a damp towel, I rubbed the white fur of their bloated tummies to stimulate defecation, but within a few days Boycat and Poep had stabilised their own toilet routine.

Lying in bed later that evening, I contemplated the complexities of Poepface's little mind. Her brother was already far more relaxed and I didn't think it would take long for him to settle down completely. But she would be a lot harder. What could I do to break through to her? There was no doubt about the fact that I had already fallen hard; Poep had captured my heart like few women ever had with her aloof, reserved nature. She was smart, enigmatic and a deep little thinker who liked to analyse a situation instead of acting on impulse. Boycat was the complete antithesis of his smaller sister. He was a placid, easy-going little man who was fine, as long as his passion for food was met and he was not interfered with at meal times. He paid me the best possible compliment when a few weeks later he gave me two puffs in greeting *knowing* that it was me and not his mother. To me, this signalled that the hardest part was behind us. But Poepface would still need time. She fell into a flat panic if she lost sight of her brother for even the shortest period of time during our early explorations in the Inyatini riverbed. Crying piteously, she would stop whatever she was doing, swivel her ears and listen intently for a response. My heart went out to her during those early days. Boycat was the last tangible thing she had left to connect her to the world that up until recently had seemed so safe.

I was only just beginning to learn how sensitive she really was.

4
HYENAS

It had been an unusually quiet night. The cubs hadn't played as much as they'd done the last three nights and I hadn't heard them since late the previous evening. Putting it down to exhaustion and the stresses of losing their mother and settling down in their new home, I parted the gauze flap of the fly screen and stepped out into a beautiful crisp morning.

The high-pitched chirps of small birds rose high over the long shadows, mixing with the rhythmic melancholic coos of Cape turtle doves and the droning of insects that filled the pre-dawn air. Tiny droplets of silvery dew clung tenaciously to the rim of the canvas roof of the tent, holding out where others had already fallen, and in the distance, north of camp, I heard a herd of elephants making their way through the bush.

Peering through the thorn scrub of the cage, I saw half a spotted tail protruding behind the cardboard box. I couldn't see much else, but felt reasonably pleased that the cubs were no longer hiding when they heard me moving around camp. As I headed towards the fireplace to put the coffee on something on the ground on the far side of the kitchen tent caught my eye, which on closer inspection turned out to be a line of rubbish that lay scattered across the ground like the random beads of a broken necklace.

Alongside were the four-toed tracks of a huge hyena. I bent down to pick up the trail of plastic bread wrappings, old teabags and punctured food cans to feel a thick, stringy layer of transparent saliva on my hands and following the trail, I found the rubbish bin a few metres away, depleted and lying on its side.

'Shit!' I cursed, trailing my finger along the bite-marks on the bin. Scolding myself for not having thought of removing all rubbish from opportunistic animals like hyenas, I somewhat grumpily turned the bin upright and started cleaning up the slimy mess, resolving to keep the bin out of reach from now on. I wasn't all that disconcerted that the hyena had come into camp, knowing they were skittish predators that would easily be scared away by a clap of the hands, but I was rather annoyed at the trail of trash I'd now have to collect. Still, I didn't like the idea of them anywhere near the cubs. Rummaging around in the storage tent for a good length of rope, I tied one end to the bin's handle, threw the other end over a sturdy branch of the marula beside the kitchen and hoisted the bin into the air, knotting the rope around the tree trunk and leaving the rubbish bin hanging like a man dangling from the gallows. Satisfied, I lowered it back down. There was a good chance the hyenas might return that night looking for more but once they realised there was nothing to be had they wouldn't linger.

A gale force wind struck up during the early hours that night. Heaving heavily beneath the howling gusts of freezing air, the tent canvas shook and bellowed. I burrowed deeper beneath the duvet and pulled an extra pair of blankets all the way over my head, surfacing every now and then to listen for any sounds from the cage. But the cubs weren't active. By early morning, the wind had died down considerably and shortly after I had finished my coffee I heard a vehicle coming down the road and pulling into camp. It was Jimmy Marshall. We hadn't had much time to catch up on each other's news recently and since we were both attending another informal film shoot with the cubs at Tetawa Dam we had agreed to drive together. After another quick cup of coffee, I walked to the cage and lifted first Boycat and then Poepface into the green travel carrier and put them on the back of my vehicle.

Driving through open woodland of *Combretum apiculatum* and *Spirostachys africana*, I steered the Land Rover west towards Tetawa Rocks, a cluster of huge granite boulders set among thick entanglements of *Acacia schweinfurthi* in a beautiful area about four kilometres from camp.

'How's Xingi, Jimmy?' I asked, realising that I'd been so preoccupied with the cubs over the last few days that I hadn't asked after Xingi when I last saw Jimmy.

Xingi, short for Xingalana, was a very sweet female lion cub who I had come to know quite well since she had been found a few months earlier by a ranger, recently abandoned by her mother. We had all known that one of the younger Sparta lionesses had been pregnant and had been anticipating the birth of the cub but, as sometimes happened with a female's first litter, she had simply walked away leaving the little cub to die in the scorching sun. It was purely by chance that the ranger came across the tiny newborn cub and when he called it over the radio to the other game guides JV had picked up the transmission on his car radio and immediately drove to fetch her. Since nature rarely takes pity on the weak or abandoned, it was a miracle that she hadn't been killed by a lion or scavenging hyena or jackal. And so she went to live with JV and Gillian in their house.

I first saw Xingi when she was just days old. Jimmy and I often went round to JV's to play with her and even when she grew bigger she still came bounding over to stalk me through the grass before launching herself with a huge thud on to my back, instinctively displaying natural behaviour that would serve her well in hunting large prey animals. When Xingi became too big and too destructive to live inside a house JV, who was capturing Xingi's progress on film, constructed a tented camp about two kilometres east of where my own camp would later be built, and moved there with

Gillian to enable Xingi to slowly adapt to the bush.

I'd only seen Xingi occasionally after that but she still recognised me even though she was now turning into quite a big girl. Greeting me affectionately, she would rub the full length of her powerful body against my legs as if welcoming a long-lost relative and although I always reciprocated her gesture, I no longer played with her quite so boisterously because I wasn't close enough to her to interpret her intentions.

Jimmy was very involved in the television documentary of Xingi, even starring in it, and it was good to hear that she was continuing to make progress. We chatted about his news and my early experiences with the cubs until we reached Tetawa Dam. Marula trees dominated the open woodland around the igneous rocks that had been formed by volcanic activity deep within the bowels of the earth millions of years ago. Molten magma, trapped in pockets, had since cooled and solidified and broken through the earth's crust to breathe a last sigh before collapsing in its final resting place. One of the larger boulders was cleaved down the middle, as though it had been struck by a giant axe and, from the very narrow opening at the front, it widened deeper into the rock into a large cave-like dwelling, which provided the perfect hiding place for vulnerable leopard cubs. The Mother Leopard had used it as a successful nursery site, as had the Tugwaan Female, her daughter from her fourth litter.

Drawing to a stop beneath the shady canopy of a tall marula several metres from the dam wall, I parked the Land Rover and got up to lift out the travel carrier, feeling the cubs wobbling about inside as I took them to where JV and Elmon were setting up their film equipment. Placing the box on top of a large fairly flat boulder I opened the door and watched as Boycat, after initial hesitation, curiously pushed his little face out and stepped on to the rock, with blue eyes sweeping from left to right and his eyes squinting slightly against the sunlight. Poepface followed close behind, peering over the boulder and padding sure-footedly along its grainy texture, sniffing here and there until they reached the opening of the cleft in the rock. Before I had the chance to avert their attention to a piece of meat, both cubs had shot straight into the opening.

'Oh, great!' My heart sank as I turned to Jimmy. 'Now what?'

Crouching down on my hands and knees, I tried to see where the cubs had gone, finding them lying huddled close together deep inside the cave as my eyes adjusted to the darkness. I tried reaching inside with the flat of my hand, moving it up and down in the hope of evoking a reaction and coaxing them out. Poepface, however, as if emboldened by her inaccessibility, merely crawled backward until she was just out of hand's reach. She looked at me and hissed, batting at my fingers with sheathed claws before retreating back to snuggle against her brother. I frowned; that hadn't worked too well. I stepped back from the opening and decided to try a different tactic. After searching for a long narrow twig I skewered a piece of meat on the tip and piled a small few pieces on the rock, dragging the meat-tipped twig along the boulder to create a scent trail. Back at the opening I poked it deep inside and wiggled it around as much as I could.

Boycat reacted instantly. Enticed by the lure of food he got up and stumbled forward towards the opening, worming his way out. Immediately catching a whiff of the trail, he nosed his way along the ground looking like an excited little boy hunting Easter eggs.

'Just keep to the right there, Graham!' JV called as he began rolling film.

In the meantime Poepface had also wriggled out of the cave and was hot on the heels of brother. In the early morning light their mottled fur blended perfectly with the grainy texture of the boulders and I could well imagine that JV captured some stunning footage.

Before long the sun broke through the soft cool air and, growing weary after the activity and excitement, the cubs slipped back into the cool shade of the rock opening where they flopped down for a little nap to escape the sun's scorching rays. Relying on Boycat's good appetite to respond to more meat once they had had their little rest, I now felt less nervous about their private space.

'Great stuff, guys,' JV said, pulling his hat further down over his eyes to shield them from the harsh sunlight. He turned to Elmon. 'I think we're pretty much done here. Let's start wrapping this up.'

After filming a few cut-away shots of the area around the dam, he started packing away his camera and, giving me the thumbs up, he and Elmon got into their vehicle and drove off.

I allowed twenty minutes of snooze time before luring Boycat towards the fissure with another chunk of meat. Grabbing him firmly by the back of the neck, I pulled him forward and free of the rock surface.

'Here,' I said turning to Jimmy, 'just hold him for me for a second.' Ignoring his slight nervousness, I handed Boycat over before bending back down to wait for Poep.

We were about halfway back to camp when we rounded a bend in the road and were taken completely by surprise to see a large male leopard padding purposefully along the right hand side of the road in our direction. It was the Sunset Bend Male, a beautiful adult leopard of about five years old that I saw only periodically. He was a relative newcomer to the reserve and had first been sighted only a year or so earlier while walking in an open area in the eastern section of the reserve called the Sunset Bend Clearing, close to Londolozi's boundary with a neighbouring reserve. This led us to believe that he had left his former home and was looking for new territory. Approaching us steadily, the Sunset Bend Male was clearly going somewhere with specific intent; his beautiful gentle eyes were focused and unflinching as he sauntered closer, stopping now and then to scrape his back feet over the ground and spray urine to scent mark the bushes. Shifting my hand slowly away from the steering wheel, I switched off the engine and we watched him approach to within a few metres. I knew that leopards had a very good sense of smell and I was interested to see how he would react to my two cubs in the back of the vehicle.

Carrying his massive body regally and padding lightly over the ground, the Sunset Bend Male drew level with us about a metre from the open side of the vehicle. Occasionally flicking his long tail at small biting flies, he appeared completely oblivious of us; if he had smelled the cubs he certainly did not let on. Continuing on our drive, Jimmy and I almost bumped into another big cat a few hundred metres before camp, one of the Dudley Pride lionesses, whose tracks we followed all the way to the bushes in front of the carport where they veered off into the undergrowth. Encounters such as these were a powerful reminder of my responsibilities and I had to wonder what the chances were of an increasing number of large predators being attracted to the smell of young leopards.

A few nights later I woke up to the whoops and lowing of a hyena a few feet in front of my tent and, sitting up slowly, I listened as the cold night air carried the calls deep into the night. Silhouetted by a near-full moon I could see her sloping body so clearly that I was virtually able to discern individual hairs on her shaggy coarse coat. Large, rounded ears were pricked in the darkness and her body appeared stiff and rigid, alert with expectancy. I watched her for a few seconds before, without anything seeming to prompt her, she suddenly took off.

In the next instant, fierce growls and snarls exploded into the night air within a hundred and fifty metres of camp as a pride of lions started squabbling over a kill. Soon other whoops, grunts and whines filled the air, leading me to believe that an entire hyena clan was mobilising in a daring bid to take over an easy meal. With cackling, high-pitched whoops and eerie giggles, the hyenas were rapidly advancing and within the next few minutes a major battle erupted over the carcass. From the volume of lion voices I was pretty sure that the Castleton Females and their eight large sub-adult cubs were defending their meal against the hyena clan. As I lay back down in bed listening to the battle between these two very different but powerful predators, I wondered what the cubs were making of the racket.

Rising at first light, I got up and stepped outside to discover two sets of huge footprints in the soft soil just before the entrance to the tent, the tracks of a single lioness and her large cub. They had walked leisurely through camp, presumably to join the rest of the pride, but I could scarcely believe that I hadn't so much as heard a sound. Two nights later, another hyena showed up in camp. By now the moon was full and round and cast a luminous metallic light over the bush enabling me to see clearly a large adult female about two feet from the fly screen. I wasn't sure if it was the same animal, but it was amazing to see her backlit. Every strand of hair, her ears and bushy tail were accentuated. With slightly parted lips, she stood listening to something my own ears failed to detect and after several minutes she turned her head to the east raising her nose to interpret the smells that lingered on the night air. Taking one or two steps forward she paused once more before loping off into the darkness. I half expected a similar scenario to the other night and waited for the eruption of another clash between hyenas and lions, but there was none and I eventually drifted back to sleep.

What seemed only minutes later I awoke a second time to hear a lioness softly moaning her contact call to another member of her pride. Anticipating a similar soft response, I kept very quiet only to be totally shaken by a lion bellowing so close by that it sounded as if he was inside the tent. Bloody hell! My eyes wide and my body tensed, I cautiously lifted my head off the pillow before slowly rolling my shoulders off the mattress to count eight shadowy shapes moving in single file in front of the fly screen. The Dudley Pride was right outside the tent, just a few feet from the canvas. It was awesome. Fascinated, I watched them, knowing that within the safety of the solid iron bars of their enclosure the cubs would be fine. Nothing short of an irate elephant bull in musth would be able to cause any damage to their cage. After a while I dozed off again, waking about an hour later to the happy sounds of Boycat and Poepface jumping on and off the cardboard box and chasing each other in circles.

It was only then that I realised that the cubs themselves were more than aware of potentially dangerous situations. Each and every time a predator had come through camp they were completely quiet, resuming their activities only once the threat had passed. For all my bush experience and acquired skills, these six-week-old leopards were far more instinctively in tune with their environment, new as it was. I had learnt something very important: that by observing and monitoring their behaviour I was far more likely to detect potential danger than by relying only on my own senses. This alleviated some of my most pressing worries.

As it was, the hyenas remained my biggest nuisance. Since hoisting the rubbish bin into the marula tree at night the incidents had been few and far between, but they soon came back. It was very early in the morning when I heard what sounded like a gunshot in the kitchen tent. I didn't want to step out into the darkness, so I lay awake until first light when I went out to find that the hyenas had struck again. An involuntary whistle escaped my lips when I bent down beside the punctured lid of the cooler box. Taking the high-density polystyrene into her jaw, the hyena had sunk her canines deep into the solid material, the pressure of which had caused the explosive sound I had heard earlier. Enough was enough; I had to start taking some drastic measures.

I asked Jackson to get me a four-metre length of chicken wire mesh which I attached across the poles at the entrance to the kitchen tent. This makeshift fence could be folded back to allow passage. Impressed by my efforts, I closed the little gate. Then, as a final touch and a bit of a joke, I put up a small cardboard sign saying 'NO HYENAS ALLOWED'. Curiously, incidents of hyena looting rarely occurred after that. I had to assume that I had either constructed a remarkably sturdy fence, or that hyenas can read.

5
DISCOVERIES AND EXPLORATIONS

Andries was a small, scrawny Mozambican in his late forties who had escaped the horrors of his war-torn country to skip the border into South Africa on foot with his brother Lawrence. Braving the perilous trek through remote, scorpion and snake infested areas of the Kruger National Park and eluding the Big Five, the two brothers went looking for a job with only the clothes on their backs. Eventually they found employment at Londolozi where they helped out with odd jobs. Modest and unassuming, Andries walked with a slight stiffness in one leg and despite his harsh features his eyes were gentle and warm. A slightly turned-up nose gave his face a pleasant appearance. Lawrence was much younger than his brother and liked to joke around. He had a nice smile, bushy hair and looked fit and lean with well-toned arms and legs. He was a hard worker, but sometimes got distracted while chatting to the other guys. Both brothers were well liked and after their arrival early in June 1993, they soon became part of the Londolozi family.

I often saw Andries fashioning grass into objects in his spare time and one day I asked him what he making. Puffing on Boxer tobacco that he had rolled in a piece of old newspaper to make a cigarette, he looked up and replied simply, '*Xibetse*'. He explained that these were bracelets which in

Shangaan tradition were customarily given as gifts. He showed me how he made them and that sparked a bright idea.

'I love them!' I said. 'They're really great. I'll tell you what ... If you teach me how to make these bracelets, I will show you how we can sell grass to white people.' He started to laugh, shaking his head in disbelief. 'No, seriously,' I told him. 'I mean it! We'll have them for sale in the curio shop. I promise you people will buy them.'

So he showed me and they sold like hot cakes.

Andries used to sleep in the storage tent when he stayed in camp to keep an eye on the cubs on the occasional night I'd drive to Main Camp to enjoy a properly cooked supper and a beer or two with some of my friends. He waived the offer to use the guest tent that had been positioned on the other side of the riverbed to provide a sense of privacy because he felt too isolated there. During the first few weeks after the cubs arrived Andries often stayed on in the morning to help out around camp. Although Boycat and Poep largely ignored him, he had a good way with the cubs and even managed to sneak in a pat here and there if Boycat walked past. On the days I asked him to keep an eye on the cubs, he either caught a lift with Jackson and Alison or asked Elmon or someone else to drop him off late in the afternoon, an hour or so before I planned to leave. I think he quite enjoyed smoking his tobacco and being in a private camp with only leopards for company, even though the storage tent provided only a metal cupboard and a bed, plus extra lanterns, blankets and other odds and ends.

'Are you going to be all right, Andries?' I asked as I made my way past the fireplace towards the carport. He nodded, waved his hand at me and said he would be fine. 'Okay, then. I'll see you later tonight. Help yourself to anything you want from the kitchen.' With that, I got into the Land Rover and drove out into the early evening.

As I went faster along the road, I felt the winter chill lash my face and hands like a whip and, while glad of my leather jacket, I felt the goosebumps growing on my bare legs. Once I was over the dam wall I saw the pretty flickering lights of Main Camp shining brightly against the night sky and, swerving around to the back of the camp I switched off the engine and rubbed my hands together to get rid of the numbness. Hoping to find Pete Short, the food and beverage manager, or Jimmy at the bar, I first popped into the office to call Cha.

A few weeks before the cubs arrived I had been managing the reserve's exclusive Tree Camp with a female colleague who had invited a friend to visit for the weekend. Charmian Supra was originally from Zambia but lived in Johannesburg where she worked as an English teacher at Wits University. We hit it off immediately and by the time Sunday afternoon arrived and Cha was preparing to leave, I knew I was in trouble.

We'd stayed in fairly regular telephonic contact and, sharing our ideas and ideals, had almost imperceptibly entered into the first fragile stages of a relationship. When I called the Johannesburg number Sally Supra, Cha's mother, answered the phone and I'd find myself chatting to her for quite some time before she eventually fetched her daughter. Today was no different. I had never met Sally but her bubbly enthusiasm ensured we were never short of words and, telling her about the leopards, I smiled at her excited responses while silently wondering what she thought of this strange man dating her lovely daughter.

My heart took a little leap when I heard Cha's soft, gentle voice. We chatted for a while and after ending our conversation I left the office to head for the bar. Pete was talking to some guests who were sitting at a beautifully laid table in the boma in front of a large fire that spat and crackled cosily as other couples filtered in to sit in a large semicircle facing the flames. Giving him a quick wave, I ordered a beer and waited at the bar for him to join me. The gentle hum of casual dinner conversations filled the early evening while every now and then a red-hot ember exploded into the air like a screaming flare. I swept my eyes over the guests. They looked like the usual clientele; generally well groomed, casually clad men and women in neutral clothing. I picked out several South African couples among the overwhelming number of international visitors enjoying a relaxing meal after an afternoon's game drive. Had they seen the Dudley Pride? Or been rewarded by a leopard sighting? From guiding experience I knew how most guests wanted to see a leopard. If they only knew ...

Sitting at the bar counter and appreciating an expertly cooked meal and a beer with Pete I realised just how lucky I was. I was living in the bush with two young leopards, with an exclusive lodge around the corner where I was served a sumptuous five-star meal. After downing a quick dessert, I told Pete I had to go. My stomach was nice and full but I suddenly had an overwhelming desire to get back to the camp and check on Boycat and Poep. I got into the Land Rover and, dimming the headlights to a soft pale glow, I manoeuvred the vehicle out of the staff car park and into the bush, penetrating the black night with powdery shafts of light and catching a glimpse of a large herd of impalas, their eyes caught shimmering in the beams. A smile curved round my lips and, relaxing behind the steering wheel, I eased into the drive. I was going home. Back to my leopards.

I HAD NEVER been a hunter or enjoyed the idea of stalking an animal to take its life, but now that I was responsible for the well-being of two leopards I was more or less required to become a killer. Leopards need meat to survive and so when impala rations ran low, I had to go out into the bush with my 30.06 calibre rifle and shoot for the cubs, much as I hated it. JV had given me two rifles, the 30.06 and a much lighter .22 that I used to hunt scrub hares at night but which was pretty much useless against anything else.

I knew exactly where all the little francolins lived and would head out early in the morning on hunting expeditions. I dreaded the idea of having to murder an innocent animal so I was determined at least to make sure that whatever I shot would never know what happened and would die instantly without pain or prolonged suffering. I gave myself plenty of target practice before going out on my first shoot and never approached a flock and blasted away, but rather tried to anticipate the direction in which they were going and run on ahead to set up an ambush. I didn't want anything to feel fear by having to stare death in the face. It'd be quick, clean and painless. I also never shot in the same area twice but spread my deadly impact around as randomly as possible, like a predator. It wasn't a nice part of my leopard responsibilities but it did sum up the essence of the bush; for something to live, something else had to die.

I'd normally shoot two or three francolins or scrub hares in a day, storing them in the gas freezer as rations for the cubs if I ran out of fresh meat. One afternoon, I had to take out a scrub hare and as I cut the frozen bunny in half I noticed two unusual round shapes on each side of the body. Pausing to stare at it for a few confused seconds, I felt horribly guilty when I realised what it was. As if it hadn't been bad enough to shoot such a cute animal, I realised that I had murdered a pregnant female. I was quite upset for some time, but was forced to accept that this was simply the darker side of my parental responsibilities.

Now that my anxieties about the cubs feeding properly had dissipated, another problem emerged. Early one morning, a day or so after our first visit to Tetawa Dam, I carried two yellow enamel bowls with neatly trimmed chunks of impala meat from Main Camp into the enclosure. With the cubs at my feet eager for their meal, I put both bowls on the ground a short distance apart. Soon afterwards, as I stepped back to sit against the mesh wall to allow them to feed in peace, Boycat stuck his fuzzy nose out to come trotting over and, diving facedown into his rations, began eating without delay. He wolfed his portion greedily, having almost finished by the time his smaller sister cautiously emerged to watch her brother feeding safely.

Emboldened, she approached to investigate her breakfast. Licking the bottom of his bowl with his little tongue, Boycat almost knocked it over and, looking up and seeing his sister feeding quietly, he lunged at her and pushed her roughly aside to steal her portion. Before I had the chance to intervene, Poepface, timid as nature had intended her to be, jumped back at him, defending her share, and before my eyes a nasty, vicious fight ensued. For a moment I was numb with shock. I couldn't believe that such small cubs could engage in such raw, savage behaviour. Boycat and Poep rolled across the ground as one ball of spitting, growling fur, biting and clawing each other and entwined with fury. I had never before seen young animals display such aggression over food and for a moment I felt helpless as to what to do. Then, darting forward, I barged in, plunging my arm down to snatch Boycat by the scruff of his neck and jerk him off the ground. He was the aggressor, and I turned him around to face me, telling him off in a stern voice.

'NO!' I said, giving him a soft smack on the nose. 'You don't steal your sister's food like that!'

But unfortunately I was to see many more of these meat fights. Sometimes the cubs got so entangled that, as I lifted Boycat into the air, he refused to release his grip and Poepface was pulled up along with him. The strangest thing of all was that when eventually the cubs relaxed and went about their business, neither of them revealed so much as a scratch, other than a patch of saliva on their fur or a tiny tuft of hair on the ground. Not once did they inflict any serious injury on each other; no scratches, open wounds or even a single drop of blood was spilt. Still, Boycat always came out on top. He was too big, too powerful and too domineering compared with his smaller sister. Once I had parted them, Poepface appeared slightly dazed, standing silently and rocking her head from side to side as her brother devoured the last of her meat. I had to do something, or that little girl would never get her fair share. So after the first few altercations I decided to separate them during mealtimes, which was quite a drastic and disconcerting option since

I knew it would definitely cause the cubs a fair measure of distress.

Since Poepface was the more sensitive, I decided to leave her in the more familiar environment of the enclosure and have Boycat feed in a spare cage we had constructed close to the fireplace. Bounding after me, he was so excited at the prospect of food that he barely noticed being in unfamiliar territory and, once inside, began feeding immediately, quite unlike his sister who, back inside the enclosure, was visibly upset. She completely ignored her bowl and cried piteously, pining for her brother. I felt awful to be the cause of her despair, but couldn't think of another way for her to get her share of food without being bullied out of it. I kept the cubs apart for no more than twenty minutes during which time Boycat too, once he'd finished eating, seemed unsettled and distressed. The cubs soon became used to this new routine, however, and the fighting diminished.

THE FOLLOWING DAY was a Friday and, waking at dawn, I sensed an extra sparkle in the fresh morning air. Cha was coming today! It was her first visit back to Londolozi after we had met at Tree Camp and I couldn't wait to show her my camp and the leopard cubs. I wondered what her reaction would be to my humble dwelling compared with the luxury she had enjoyed during her last visit and how she would respond to the leopards. It was entirely normal for anyone to feel a little nervous around them for, although they were still small, Boycat and Poep were leopards after all and pretty intimidating little cats. Hoping to get the three off to a good start, I left Cha sitting by the dormant fireplace while I went to the cage to open the door to let Boycat and Poep out.

'Don't pay them any specific attention, Cha,' I advised her as I unlatched the lock to the enclosure and stepped in. 'If they want to come up to you, just let them. They'll discover you at their own pace.'

Poepface was far from impressed. She stayed at the far side of the camp, giving Cha a distrustful, disdainful stare which Cha gracefully ignored. Although Cha and I had not yet come to know each other all that well, she intuitively sensed the depth and intensity of the feelings I had for the cubs, even during those very early days. It couldn't have been easy for Cha to be with someone whose priorities had to lie elsewhere. Yes, we were at the cusp of something special, but I wasn't entirely consumed by the overwhelming romantic feelings most couples go through during the early days of a new relationship. I couldn't be. I lived in a different world. So much so that even if the cubs *had* pounced on her I probably would have taken up their cudgels. And Cha knew that.

But nothing happened. The dynamics between Cha and the cubs were on a completely different level from what they were to me, but she was good with them and Boycat, oblivious of his sister's resentment towards this petite woman with the short blonde hair, immediately flirted his way into her heart. It was the first time I was properly able to assess the cubs' behaviour towards a visitor, someone other than the people they had seen working around camp, such as Jackson and Alison. In time to come I was able to witness an uncanny ability on their part to virtually read any person like a book, and that included me. If the cubs detected an inkling of hesitation, apprehension or fear in someone, they immediately ganged up on that person with Boycat usually taking the lead. He would appear in full view, while Poep sneaked up from behind. And so the cubs approached in a pincer movement to harass their victim mercilessly. Together, like two playground bullies, they wickedly delighted in terrorising the fearful person. Oddly enough, if the visitor displayed no fear, Boycat and Poep were on their best behaviour and showed no malicious intent whatsoever.

It was on the morning that Cha arrived that I made my first proper breakthrough with Poep. It was almost two weeks since the cubs had arrived in camp and Boycat had slowly started to settle down. He responded to my chuffs every morning in the happy knowledge it was me and, raising his tail all the way over his back, he'd squint a little as he peered at my face in the early sunlight. But Poepface was not that easy to get through to. Her terror lingered and her highly-strung character and nervousness struck a profound chord within me. I still spent many hours each day sitting inside the enclosure with my back to the mesh watching her pacing, seemingly oblivious to the fact that she actually moved through the tunnel-like passage that my raised knees provided. Her features reflected her confusion; she was in her own private nightmare and barely acknowledged my presence. Her behaviour had plagued me for days, but today I could bear it no longer. The next time she brushed past me I quickly lifted her up by the scruff of her neck and daringly set her on my lap and began to massage her gently behind the ears. She stiffened instantly, but after one or two seconds I felt her rigidity ease as my fingers moved in circular motions over the tense muscles in her neck. It didn't last long, perhaps no more than fifteen seconds, before she jumped away, but it was a start.

THE WEEKEND WAS great and had stirred some powerful emotions. Any doubts from my side before she arrived were dispelled when Cha prepared to leave on Sunday morning. She had taken sleeping in the freezing cold tent with whooping hyenas close by and two leopards and a madman for company completely in her stride. Both of us were a little upset when the time came to drive her back to Main Camp, where she had left her own car, to begin the six-hour journey to Johannesburg. It seemed impossible. She, an English teacher with a structured lifestyle and me, living with leopards in the heart of the bush. And yet I had a good feeling about us.

When I arrived back in camp several hours later, I unlatched the door to the enclosure, leaving it slightly ajar so that the cubs could emerge and explore the camp at their leisure. Earlier, I'd dug a fairly deep hole and planted a large dead tree trunk in it which I'd stabilised with heavy rocks and large stones, thus creating a small tree which I hoped would stimulate the cubs' interest and stop them from wanting to explore further away. They loved the tree and often sat in the fork of the trunk overseeing camp activities, watching for any movements and listening to the calls of the bush.

Boycat was the first to come out of the enclosure and, padding curiously into the kitchen tent, he stood still between the rolled-up canvas flap peering to left and right before getting the fright of his life when his tail knocked a broom to the floor. He cowered in a half-crouch, pulling his lips into a snarl and hissing loudly at the unexpected noise. Alert and watchful for a few seconds, he regained his composure and moved steadily forward with Poepface following close behind. Sweeping their bright blue eyes over the kitchen's interior, the cubs sniffed every object thoroughly before moving on to the next. After pawing at the table's unresponsive legs they trudged on to find some enamel plates and mugs stacked in a small pile on top of a small cardboard box.

Satisfied, the cubs marched back towards the tent opening where Poep paused to investigate the mysterious space created by the flap folded back against the canvas. Raising her head and looking for the best angle, she jumped in, lying down as if it were a hammock, seemingly enjoying being tucked away. In the meantime, her brother was trudging back alongside the cage towards my tent. He paused at my gym bench, sniffing the weights and other gym equipment in front of the tent before pushing his face between the loosely hanging open flaps and stumbling in. Flip-flops, a few scattered clothes and the bedside table were investigated and approved of, as was the cupboard and the space beneath the bed. Poepface, having leapt out of the flap shortly after discovering it, joined her brother inside my tent and together they shuffled under the bed, where they appeared to want to have a little rest.

Scrambling out a little later, Poepface eyed the soft bedding and without too much hesitation, she jumped on to the blankets and felt her way towards the pillow. Apparently enjoying the softness it provided, she promptly lay down and looked around the tent before putting her head down.

'Such a clever little girl,' I whispered, ecstatically happy to see her so relaxed. I was nowhere near her heart yet, but seeing her without that haunted look I had come to know so well I felt as though, as of today, we were heading in the right direction.

Poep in playful mood as she explores the crane

The cubs inspect the equipment

Poep taking Leppe for a walkabout

Around the fireplace with the camp staff. Image courtesy Paul Gibbons

Big cuddles for Boycat. Image courtesy Mr Cooke

Love and cuddles for Poepity too

Poep gets airborne in the Masai-Mara – to Boycat's amazement.
Image courtesy Heather Samuels

Poep under my bed after a successful shoe hunt

Poep surveys the camp from the fork in the marula tree

The cubs investigate Karin's soap dish on the tree stump. Image courtesy Paul Gibbons

The cubs and I winding down after a morning walk. Image courtesy Mark Tennant

Poep batting my hand. Image courtesy Mark Tennant

Boycat upends Karin's green bucket. Image courtesy Paul Gibbons

Poep in her tent ambush spot

Boycat needs comforting after the goat attack in the manyatta when the Maasai were after his blood

6
KARIN

Predator activity remained pretty constant around camp for the following few days. Lions had been calling for four consecutive nights and one evening while I was making supper in the kitchen tent I heard muffled footsteps close to the other side of the canvas wall. Quickly grabbing the paraffin lamp I stepped under one half-dropped flap and shone the softly flickering flame into the darkness, catching two hyenas prowling around the rubbish bin. Holding out the lamp to shine it ahead I caught sight of one jumping on top of the lid with a thud. Hoisting the bin into the tree was my last task before bedtime and since it was only about 7.30pm, I was surprised that they were sniffing around this early. Indignantly, I slapped my thigh a few times. 'HEY! HEY!' I yelled. The hyenas bolted immediately and I closed the makeshift fence around the kitchen entrance a little earlier than usual.

Perhaps, I thought, thinking back to my conversation with JV a few days earlier, he was right and it would be a good idea to have another person permanently in camp to help me look after the cubs. Up to then only Andries or Lawrence had stayed over some nights when I visited Main Camp. I have always been a private person and couldn't suppress some mixed feelings when JV first raised the issue with me. The camp had become my home and I wasn't sure how I'd feel about sharing my space with someone I had never even met. All I knew was that her name was Karin Slater, that she was a friend of one of the rangers, came from a farming background and had recently graduated from film school, which was probably why JV thought she was the right person for the job. I was less sure. My greatest and most worrying concern was about her lack of bush knowledge. It was one thing to start training as a novice game guide and learning to read the signs of the bush and animal behaviour from the safety of a vehicle, but quite another to simply drive up from town, unpack your bags and settle into a tent with lions, elephants and hyenas moving freely around the environment. You needed vigilance, an intricate understanding of wild animals and a certain amount of practical bush experience, and as far as I knew she had none of these. Rather than an asset, she could well prove more of a liability. My equally pressing concern was that her priorities regarding the cubs might be very different from mine.

My first impressions of Karin were that she was very tall, very arty, very laid back, very enthusiastic and that she had the biggest feet I'd ever seen on a woman, which is why, perhaps a little unkindly, I started calling her Big Foot. But she was a nice person with a good sense of humour and didn't mind my nickname for her. Genuinely excited to be in the bush, she followed me through camp as I showed her around, explaining the workings of the kitchen, the loo and water cart, and warning her about the potter wasps that had made a nest inside the shower head. I left her to settle into her tent behind the fireplace while deliberating how best to introduce her to Boycat and Poep and came to the conclusion that it was probably best if she forged her own relationship with them, which she did over time. She became very close to Boycat, perhaps even closer than I did over the months, because, much as I loved my little man, I felt compelled to break through to Poepface. Still, we couldn't have been more different. While I couldn't wait to jump out of bed to spend time with the cubs, Karin regularly overslept in the mornings, which was fine, except that I couldn't comprehend anyone who'd rather lie in bed than get up at first light to spend time with two young leopards.

For the first few days I urged Karin to adopt a passive approach towards the cubs as they were walking freely through camp during the day. I still strongly believed that the best way to get through to them was to let them get used to a new person in their own time. Even now, after twenty-one days, Poep still slunk behind the cardboard box when she heard me approach the enclosure and only emerged from cover after I had chuffed at her.

The daily routine of morning and afternoon explorations in the donga continued with Karin now joining us. We returned to camp an hour or two before midday when the heat became too much to bear and, although I still occasionally put Boycat and Poep inside the enclosure for a lunchtime nap, they felt confident enough in camp to follow me to my tent to enjoy snoozing with me on the bed. During one of our lazy lunchtime naps I caught Boycat hiccuping himself to sleep after having gobbled his breakfast too fast. I thought my heart would burst with tenderness.

Those were some of our best times. Every morning I'd find two little leopards eager let be out. Poep still liked to follow her brother's lead but where he was the braver of the two, she beat him with her incredible agility and precision. Boycat was a typical rumbustious little boy, crashing around like a runaway bus and always wanting to be part of the action. She remained more reserved and analytical, observing things before responding to them. More often than not, I broke into a playful run as we approached camp after our morning walk and, bounding after me, the cubs chased me all the way across the sandy floor of the riverbed. Glancing back and seeing two small leopards excitedly trying to keep up with me was one of the most incredible experiences of my life.

At the end of the day it was the cubs themselves who were in charge. I always gauged their behaviour to assess where to go and how far. They always had the choice and Karin and I would simply follow. If Boycat or Poep showed any signs of fatigue I'd take the initiative to head back to they were preoccupied by new scents or clearly determined to do their own thing, I would sit close by and watch them, waiting for them to give me the signal they had grown tired. Our explorations in the bush were never rigid or timed; I didn't wear a watch and I was keen to allow their instincts to rise to the surface. This was not always an easy thing for Karin to understand in the beginning as she had no knowledge of leopard behaviour. A dilating or narrowing pupil, swivelling of the ears, a flick of a tail or twitching whiskers – all these subtle signs were important clues which foretold a change of mood that, if ignored, could result in a potentially dangerous situation.

Not surprisingly, Boycat was an easier cat to read than Poep, although he also had his grumpy moments. Sometimes I tried to alleviate these by deliberately tripping him up and, quickly flicking him on to his side, I would run my hand between his back legs and rub the soft white fur of his tummy. He loved it, keeling over instantly and relishing the attention. Poepface wasn't always in the mood to be stroked and if I tried the same tactics of tripping her up she became irritated, flipping herself back on to all fours and walking away in a huff. Sometimes she turned after a few paces, striking the air with her paw as if to say, 'I'll play with you, but only when I want to and on my terms.'

My main concern for Karin was that she might compromise her own safety by overstepping the cubs' personal boundaries. Although they were only nine weeks old, Boycat and Poep wore some dangerous ammunition in the form of dagger-like claws and very sharp little teeth. I had stupidly wanted to test the strength of those teeth and jaws a few days after the cubs arrived and allowed Poep to bite me twice on the hand when I tried feeding her with the bottle. The pain that shot up my arm was excruciating. And I was still more than a little concerned about Karin's general lack of bush knowledge and wild animals. The area around camp was a potentially dangerous place and if she reacted in the wrong way in a situation involving a large animal, it could end fatally.

Only two days earlier, one of the Dudley Males had come into camp in the middle of the night, venturing to within an arm's reach of my tent two or three hours after I had gone to sleep. Lying on my side, I had buried my head deep beneath the blankets with only my nose sticking out for air in an attempt to ward off the freezing cold when deep rhythmic breathing, out of sync with my own, roused me from sleep. My first thought was that I had been dreaming, but something made me keep still and listen. Within a split second I knew there was a lion right outside and that I'd better keep dead still because he had to be damn close if I'd been able to hear his breathing so clearly.

My head was more or less resting against the fly screen at the back of the tent and since I kept both sides of the canvas up, there wasn't much material between the two of us. With his impeccable night vision, the lion could easily see me through the mesh. Very slowly, I began pulling the blanket away from my eyes, centimetre by centimetre so as not to cause any sudden movement that might provoke an attack. I had no doubt in my mind that a lion could easily burst straight through the flimsy screen and take my head off. From the sound of it, his mouth was very close to my head and I could smell his breath, strong and musty like that of an old carcass. Peeling the duvet off just far enough to enable me to see, my eyes slowly adjusted to the silvery light to reveal a massive head framed by a luxurious long mane. Illuminated by a full moon, I recognised one of the Dudley Males. He was so close that I saw the steam of his breath as he exhaled.

For about two or three heart-stopping minutes that seemed to last for ever, I waited as he slowly moved his head three-quarters of the way towards me, peering at the corner of the tent in the direction of the cubs' enclosure. I wondered if he had picked up their scent but, not comprehending the notion of a cage, couldn't work out where they were. Then he took a step to the left and walked off at an oblique angle, his long heavy body and taut belly sliding past in the light, to disappear silently into the bush in a north-easterly direction. I almost had to pinch myself to be sure it had happened, but I revelled in the riveting experience of having a lion pass by so closely. Unike Karin, I knew lion behaviour. If I hadn't had the awareness to keep dead still and not panic, it could all have gone pretty much pear-shaped. Any sudden movements and he could easily have burst in and bitten my head off. A shiver ran down my spine. What if he had stopped beside Karin's tent? With her lack of bush knowledge, would she have had the presence of mind not to react?

When JV came round later that morning, I told him about my misgivings. 'What if she comes across the Dudleys on foot?' I asked. 'Or gets charged by an elephant? God knows, anything could happen.'

JV nodded, lowered his head in thought and rubbed his chin. As a man with a deep-seated affinity for the bush and all its creatures and with his many years' experience, he understood the dangers all too well.

'Can you teach her to use a rifle, Graham? At least that way she'll have some sort of protection.'

I agreed with him and figured that the sooner I did this the better. So later that morning, when the cubs had gone back inside the enclosure following their walk, Karin and I went to the donga for some target practice. We headed down the bank towards an open stretch of sand about 200 metres from my tent, and stopped before a wide bend. Satisfied with the location, I held out the two weapons I had brought; the .22 and the much heavier 30.06 calibre rifle that JV had given me a while back.

Starting her off on the lighter weapon, I put the 30.06 down on the sand and stuffed a handful of bullets into the pockets of my shorts.

'Okay,' I said, holding out the rifle, 'this is where we start.' I pointed to the top of the rifle. 'You open the bolt by lifting it up and pulling it back. This will get rid of any cartridges still left in the breech, also called the firing chamber … like so.' With a click, I opened the bolt and showed her the empty chamber, handing over the rifle so that she could get a feel for it. 'Then,' I continued, 'once you have physically checked and double-checked that there are no more bullets or rounds left in the chamber and you know the weapon is safe, you can start loading it. But first, let's practise holding and aiming for a bit.'

Never one to underestimate the sheer destructive power of firearms, I took my time taking her through the motions before allowing her to actually handle the rifle herself.

'Now, this is how you stand.' Planting my feet firmly on the ground just over shoulder-width apart, I had Karin do the same while holding the rifle at arm's length.

After a bit of practice, I pulled a few bullets out of my pocket and held one of them up in front of her. 'See? You take a round and put it into the magazine like this … the magazine clips back into place when you leave the breech open.'

Demonstrating the procedure carefully, I held the bolt back and slid one bullet into the firing chamber, then closed it by lowering the bolt again. 'The weapon is now considered loaded, or cocked, and is ready to fire. Remember,' I reiterated, 'a loaded weapon, is a dangerous weapon!' As she watched, I unloaded the rifle and handed it back to her to practise this next step.

Talking her through the procedure, I watched her load the rifle correctly. 'Right. Now for the target …' I took the loaded rifle from her and picked up an old cardboard box I had found in the kitchen which I placed on the ground about ten paces away. Giving the rifle back to her, I said, 'Take aim as I showed you and keep your eye on the sight, as that is where the bullet will hit.' Watching her closely, I stepped back a metre or so and let her take her first shot.

Inhaling somewhat tensely, Karin tilted back her dark brown floppy hat, expertly closed one eye and pulled the trigger. With a small pop, the bullet exploded from the muzzle and perforated the cardboard leaving a tidy, round hole the size of a medium-sized marble. Perfect! Taking aim once more, she fired again, shooting about five rounds before looking up triumphantly. She had a natural flair and I was quite impressed.

'Okay,' I said, 'very good. Now you check again that the chamber is free from the round.' I took the rifle from her and after taking aim at the box with the 30.06 to show her what to expect, I handed Karin the much more powerful rifle. 'Now try this one. But remember, it's a lot more powerful.'

Holding the 30.06 slightly awkwardly, Karin appeared to be struggling a bit so I took it back and demonstrated how to really lean into it, pushing the butt of the rifle into the curve of her shoulder to create more balance in her upper body. 'That should also protect you from the recoil,' I told her. 'Here, try it.'

After practising for a while, she seemed more relaxed with the firearm. I handed her a round of bullets, oversaw her loading the rifle and take aim once again. A few doves burst from their perches in the nearby trees as the rifle blasted solidly into the air. Turning to me, Karin raised her eyebrows in surprise. 'Wow!' She seemed quite exhilarated by the kick and was eager to fire another four or five rounds, all of which she got pretty much on target. Although I couldn't be sure of her natural reaction to any sudden situation where she would have to defend herself, at least I felt better about having to leave the cubs for a town visit the following morning. It would be the very first time that I had been away from them since they arrived three weeks earlier and, after only a week in camp, I hoped Karin would be able to handle it.

A STABBING PAIN at the back of my mouth had woken me before dawn the previous morning and, groaning, I lifted my hand to cradle my left cheek. I'd felt the early stirrings of a painful wisdom tooth for the past few days but, like most neurotic new parents, I hadn't wanted to leave the cubs for an entire day with Andries or Lawrence in order to have it checked out by a dentist in town. However, as it turned out, I had to get to a hardware store to buy some welding gloves because JV was worried that Karin might get her arms and legs ripped during playful interactions with the cubs. Taking the opportunity to kill two birds with one stone, I asked someone at Main Camp to phone a dentist to make an appointment before infection set in.

Swinging the Land Rover around the dam wall, I pulled into the Main Camp's staff car park and made my way to the reception area to meet Melly, who I knew was also going into Nelspruit that morning. Melly Piëst was a British girl who had come to South Africa after a six-month overland journey from London to Johannesburg in 1982, the realisation of a lifelong dream. As a young girl Melly had had a deep-seated love for wildlife, often sitting up late with her dad to watch wildlife documentaries on television. When she took a break from her work in children's homes in the UK to travel through Africa, she fell in love with wild animals all over again. From observing gorillas in the Rwandan Virungu Mountains to driving amongst lions, giraffes and wildebeest in spectacular wildlife areas such as the Masai Mara and the Ngorongoro Crater, Melly took the plunge and made a permanent move to Johannesburg, taking every opportunity she could to visit the bush.

After a one-night stay with friends at Londolozi in 1984, Melly was captivated and eventually, three years later, she took up a position as housekeeper at Main Camp in early 1987 before starting work at reception, and then front of house and guest relations officer. I first met her when I was starting out as a young inexperienced game guide in 1989 and we hit it off immediately. I liked her outgoing, vibrant and enthusiastic personality and appreciated the fact that she could laugh at my wicked sense of humour, something not everyone did. We had great fun at staff parties, always sharing a laugh, and soon became great friends.

There were one or two other staff members already inside the microbus combi when we climbed in and, giving the driver the thumbs-up as the last passengers to arrive, we sat back to exchange news and enjoy the ride. Twenty minutes later we reached the Kingston Gate, the border with the outside world, and rattled along the gravel road for about ten kilometres before we reached the tarred R536, which stretched for another 37 or so kilometres into the small town of Hazyview. From there, the road wound through an undulating terrain of tree-covered hills and granite outcrops with occasional mud-walled hut communities scattered on the hillsides. The charcoal factory loomed in the distance and after we had passed it, the landscape began opening up into much flatter areas of expansive grassland that supported an increasing number of settlements of brick houses. Men and women walked along the side of the road, the women in colourful attire and balancing firewood, bags of maize flour and groceries on their cloth-covered heads.

We turned left onto the R40, passing the banana plantations on the outskirts of town that made way for long stretches of commercial pine and blue gum. I always felt a little unsettled seeing these alien tree species, imagining what the landscape must have looked like before people destroyed the natural habitat and the rich biodiversity of life that once existed there. Fifty kilometres further on we rolled into the suburbs of the relatively large town of Nelspruit. People were everywhere, traipsing like busy ants along neat pavements, past shops and impressive office buildings. Many of them were game and agricultural farmers, dressed in khaki shirts and shorts and stocking up on supplies, but there were also housewives and office workers and the occasional visitor en route to the Kruger Park or private reserves.

The microbus stopped in the middle of town and its occupants spilled out. Agreeing to meet Melly in an hour and a half, I made my way to the dentist who had his practice in an old brick building that for some reason reminded me of an old-fashioned fire station. After reporting to the receptionist, I took a seat in a tiny waiting room crammed with patients, my long legs butting into a low coffee table covered with a scattering of magazines. Some of the patients looked anxious, but others simply seemed bored.

When my turn came I was almost grateful for the piercing stab of the injection, which soon rendered the left side of my cheek completely numb. Lying back in the chair, I felt some dull, distant sensation as the dentist used various instruments to investigate and then extract the tooth. It offered some resistance but eventually it came out with a crunching sound. This was followed up with a few stitches and a swab to clean up the mess. It was over. Moving my tongue over the left upper row of teeth it slipped into what felt like a huge cavity. Shivering a little with relief, I got up, thanked the dentist and settled the bill with the receptionist, giving her a somewhat lopsided smile.

Next stop was the hardware store and once back on the street I thought of Boycat and Poep. What were they doing now? They were just 120 kilometres away, but I felt as if I had left them in another world. It was strange to think of the camp and the donga while standing in the middle of a crowded town. I'd been away from them for barely more than a few hours and already I was missing them badly. I imagined Poepface being let out of the enclosure by Karin and following her and Andries down to the dry riverbed, wary, unsure and remote. Despite her apparent disdain for people I knew that all she wanted was to be understood, for someone to reach below the surface of her complex mind.

Stopping for a quick bite at the Baghdad Café, I clumsily slurped the contents of a lime milkshake as the sedation slowly wore off, while Melly enjoyed the luxury of choosing between menu items like pizzas, burgers and other food we didn't normally get to eat. The Irish coffee we both ordered as dessert definitely made up for the scanty lunch and, armed with our shopping, we got into the bus and set off on our way back to Londolozi.

It was about 3pm when we arrived back at Main Camp. I had last seen the cubs the previous evening when I checked on them before nightfall; it seemed more like week ago. Although I was never one to stay in town for long, something was different this time. It wasn't just about how much better I felt in the bush, it was because I had two little leopards who depended on me.

7
WINTER

The sun had lost some of its afternoon strength as we pulled up in front of Main Camp and, not wanting to waste any time, I grabbed the plastic bag with the welding gloves and after bidding Melly a somewhat hasty goodbye, I hurried to the staff car park. A train of dust rose in my wake as I drove along the edge of the airstrip, down Strip Road and across the Xabene riverbed to climb over the rise and round the last corner into camp. The Land Rover ground to a stop beneath the shade of the carport and, not wanting to miss out on another walk, I jumped out of the vehicle and followed the tracks left behind by Karin, Andries and the cubs on their way to the donga. They were a few hundred metres to the east and I quickly caught up with them. I was slightly out of breath and still anxious about being away from them, but Boycat and Poep just looked at me with a rather quizzical expression as if to say *Oh, there you are!* as I drew up alongside them.

We walked down the bank together, watching Boycat pause to sniff at a short, thorny bush while Poep busied herself batting at a small stick with the soft padding of her right front paw. Allowing Boycat and Poep to set the pace, the three of us followed the cubs as they picked up a scent trail on the sandy riverbed. Suddenly, a low raspy growl rose from the undergrowth about twenty metres to our right. The cubs immediately locked on to the direction of the sound. Poepface froze, instinctively heeding the calls of a fellow leopard. Arching her back stiffly, she remained rooted to the spot for a few seconds while pulling her ears back flat against her head. Then, as if seeking solace, she pressed her little tummy to the ground and, lowering herself into a half crouch, trotted towards me. Boycat, who was closer to Karin and Andries, appeared much less intimidated. He merely swivelled his ears to tune in to the unfamiliar sound, as if more curious than anything else, and listened intently.

Narrowing my eyes, I too listened carefully and swept my eyes over the bush. Was it the Tugwaan Female? This was, after all, her core area. But then I figured that if there was an adult leopard around Boycat wouldn't have reacted in quite such a relaxed way. And the Tugwaan Female wouldn't be sticking around but would have quietly slipped back into the bush without giving herself away by growling. No, I thought, it must be one of her two ten-month old daughters, who she had given birth to in August the previous year. The Tugwaan Female had raised her cubs in the vicinity of a rocky area a kilometre or so upstream from camp, after successfully rearing her first litter of cubs to adulthood four years earlier. They were the gorgeous male and female Carlson and I had first seen as tiny cubs shortly after I arrived at Londolozi. I had no idea where they were today, but figured they had probably sought and since established their own territories on a neighbouring reserve. Bumping into any leopard on foot was extremely dangerous, but taking into account Tugwaan's fiery personality and the fact that she might not be far away from what I believed was one of her daughters seemed like a death wish at the end of a long tiresome day. Perhaps she heard us, or had been watching us from cover. Whatever the reason, the growls stopped and only the tranquil melodic cooing of doves and the cheeping of small birds hovered in the cool afternoon air.

Back at camp, after an early supper of spuds blackened in the fire with charcoal bits for spice I turned in and mulled over the events of the day.

Poep had stolen my heart when she had come to me to be comforted and I really felt that my efforts were beginning to pay off at last. Boycat was so much more laid back and generally fairly easy going with the others during our film shoots, but there was something very special about Poep. Her emotions ran so deep; it made me feel quite special that she appeared to trust me more than anyone else. Perhaps we were similar in some ways. I understood her need to be left alone without being fussed over and the way she analysed people before trusting them enough to become friendly with them. She still growled at me sometimes when she was irritated or tired but she no longer lashed out at me, trying to swat me with her paw. Perhaps she was finally beginning to realise that I was sensitive to her moods and respected them.

I had just fallen asleep when I woke to the sound of an impala calling the alarm not far from camp. Sitting up in bed, I rubbed my eyes. Before the cubs arrived I'd sleep like the dead, but now I slept with one ear open, heeding the slightest sound. All those extra pairs of eyes were of immeasurable value to me. Propped on my elbows, I stared into the moonless night and waited, but when the calling stopped I slid back down and relaxed once more. False alarm perhaps, I thought, pushing my feet deeper into the blankets and lying down flat on my back.

On my way to make coffee the following morning, I stopped abruptly when I saw drag marks along the side and front of the kitchen tent. A patch of smudged sand, resembling that of someone hauling a sack too heavy to carry along the ground, and one set of leopard paw prints were visible on the ground between the cubs' enclosure and my tent, passing straight through camp past the spare cage and down into the donga. Following the paw prints into the riverbed and up the opposite side of the bank, I trailed along for about ten metres until I noticed the rather dismal remains of an adult impala ram dangling from the branches of a sturdy leadwood like a threadbare coat flapping in the wind. Two other, slightly smaller, sets of leopard tracks emerged from the bush to join the drag marks. So it had been the Tugwaan Female lurking in the vicinity of the camp after all! Studying her tracks, I suspected that after killing the impala in the bush behind camp, she had dragged her heavy prey towards her two daughters, who had been waiting for their mother on the opposite side of the donga. Looking up at the leathery stringy lengths of meat, and the few tufts of fur that a light breeze had blown on to a thorny bush, I couldn't help wondering if these were the remains of the very impala I'd heard earlier that morning, snorting the alarm too late.

Making sure the three leopards were no longer in the immediate vicinity of camp, I went back with some dry kindling to get a fire going and filled the black iron kettle with water from the cart to make coffee. Since Karin was still asleep and since there were no sounds coming from the enclosure, I took time to enjoy the early morning. A band of clouds was rolling in and, hoping the morning's film shoot at Mbavala Rocks might be cancelled, which usually happened when the light was dull and grey, I unlatched the lock of the enclosure and waited for two small leopard faces to appear. But, unusually, Boycat wasn't all that keen to come out. Again, I thought, this was probably because the cubs had been more than aware of the Tugwaan Female feeding nearby with her two daughters. It was only when I peered inside the enclosure that Boycat, enticed by the yellow enamel bowl, cautiously stuck his face around the corner of the door and followed me somewhat warily to the spare cage where I left him to feed in peace. Then, after giving Poep her breakfast inside the enclosure, I heard a crackling voice calling me over the radio in the kitchen tent and hastily made my way back to retrieve the microphone from the handset.

'Come in, JV.' After waiting for the few seconds of static to settle I heard JV's voice on the other end.

'Graham, Duncan's vehicle broke down on his way over to our camp. I've organised some guys to come out from Main Camp and am headed out there now. The shoot is cancelled. Do you copy? The shoot is cancelled this morning. We'll continue the shoot later this afternoon.'

Secretly pleased, I pressed the button on the side of the mike and replied, 'Thanks, JV. Got that. Over and out.'

DUNCAN MCLAUGHLIN HAD come to Londolozi to do a bit of filming for JV when Xingi was about five months old. He had been recruited as the director of photography for the film 'Running Wild' in which the cubs would star. In his thirties, I had found Duncan to be a gentle, kind-hearted man who was a masterful storyteller and possessed a great sense of humour. He exploded with creativity and at times I could literally see his mind racing with new ideas. Yet he also had his moments of quiet reflection. The only area where we clashed was over the cubs.

At times I felt that Boycat and Poepface were kept waiting on set far too long while Duncan prepared the scene. As we were filming in different locations around the reserve this meant they were kept inside the travel carrier until I was told to let them out. I appreciated the fact that every minute or roll of tape was costing a lot of money, but my main concern was for the cubs' well-being and I couldn't, wouldn't, jeopardise or compromise the fledgling trust I had managed to build with them. Although Boycat had settled down well, he still had his moments and I didn't want to risk losing the trust that had slowly developed between us. After almost a month Poepface remained wary and aloof and I spent hours awake each night, wondering how I could break through that wall of fear and uncertainty she had built around herself. The expression in her eyes haunted me every day, so pandering to the perfect shot was the last thing on my mind. People seemed sometimes to forget that these were small leopards and, although cute beyond belief, they weren't pets. Boycat's easy-going nature, coupled with his love for food, usually ensured that we could successfully manipulate him to act out little scenes with the lure of meat, but Poepface could never be directed or expected to listen to commands, as Duncan was soon to find out.

Driving through thick riverine bush a few kilometres past Tetawa Dam towards the southern boundary of the reserve, I rattled along the dirt road with the cubs in their carrier towards Mbavala Rocks later that afternoon for another shoot. A little further on the area opened up with sweeping guinea grass carpeting the clearing and scattered raisin bushes and weeping wattles. I finally came to a standstill in the shade of a tall weeping wattle near two massive granite rocks.

Always a bit unsettled on unfamiliar terrain, Poep remained close behind her brother as he tottered along the coarse rock surface with Duncan filming the sequence from a short distance away. After a few minutes he stopped rolling his tape and raised his head to look around, opting to move his tripod to a different position to film from a different angle. He came over to explain where he wanted the cubs, but as he approached Boycat and Poep, he failed to read the frown-like furrow in the middle of Poep's forehead and walked straight up to her. Already mildly irritated, she watched him draw close and, reacting to his outstretched arm that was meant to guide her and her brother into the frame of his lens, she shot her head forward and clamped her mouth over his hand, biting down hard on his finger.

'*AUUUGGHHH!*' Duncan's eyes grew wide with shock and, yelping loudly, he quickly pulled his hand away. I winced for him, knowing the strength of her jaws but I also understood that it was the only way she could let him know that he had overstepped the mark. Unfortunately for Duncan, he didn't know how to interpret these subtle signs and received a second painful reminder an hour or two later at the Tree House.

A few weeks earlier a small group of workers, including Andries and Lawrence, had begun constructing a wooden cabin in the canopy of a magnificent big jackalberry tree, about 100 metres west of my camp. Although not yet finished, the set had taken on the appearance of a proper tree house, one in which I wouldn't have minded spending the rest of my life. I started walking the cubs there about a fortnight earlier on those mornings when they wanted to explore in that direction, reckoning it would be a good thing for them to familiarise themselves with the set and to explore the scattered building materials and early scaffolding.

I followed the dirt road that had been constructed when building had begun, to arrive in the open clearing where JV, Duncan and Elmon were setting up their gear on the main deck of the tree house. Calling the cubs to follow me up the long, wooden swing bridge they started investigating every nook and cranny before Duncan signalled he was ready to start filming. The scene called for JV and Elmon to bottle feed the cubs and, seated on the ground, both men waited for Boycat and Poep to come past before lifting them cautiously by the scruff of the neck. JV got hold of Boycat while Elmon reached for Poep and as they brought the bottles to their lips, Duncan started filming. Having long since stopped drinking like this, Boycat and Poep began resisting, struggling to take the milk, gnawing at the teat and boxing the plastic with their front paws.

Complaining in a high-pitched croaky voice, Poep wailed when she was let go, her chin dripping with white liquid. Duncan smiled; he had the perfect shot. Walking over to give her a friendly rub on the head, he had forgotten her earlier reaction to him. Staring with open hostility, Poep grabbed his hand and bit him once more, resentful at being manipulated and at the uncalled-for familiarity. I felt a bit sorry for Duncan; he genuinely liked animals and only wanted to be nice, but Poepface wasn't interested and resisted being touched by anyone. When she came looking for me a little later she found me sitting quietly in a corner while Duncan and JV were discussing how to tackle the next scene. She blinked tiredly and, increasing her pace, wobbled towards me on her stumpy legs. Snuggling against my legs, she raised her little head and rested her face in the hollow of my hand. With her whiskers tickling my bare skin, I felt her breathing slow until she fell asleep with her head in my hands.

'OKAY, GRAHAM,' DUNCAN announced at the following day's shoot. 'We're good to go. Ready when you are.'

'Okay,' I nodded. 'I'm ready.'

Bending his head, Duncan brought his eye down over the viewfinder of his camera. 'Right ... and ... *ACTION!*'

As per his instructions, I picked Boycat up and, in one long swoop, hurled him straight into the soft fabric of a hammock about a metre from where I was standing, making sure I was well out of frame. A few seconds later Poepface sailed through the air to land beside her brother.

'AND CUT!' Duncan yelled. 'Perfect. Thanks, Graham.'

It was all a big game for the cubs. Boycat looked up with bright shining eyes, as if he wanted to do it again. Of course, on reviewing the footage it seemed as if the cubs had jumped into the hammock of their own accord. Offering first Boycat and then Poep their rewards, my little girl seized her francolin firmly between her jaws and carried it away to a quiet corner to start feeding unaware that Boycat was eyeing her from the other side of the deck. Suddenly he dropped his Cape turtle dove and, in a few fast bounds, rushed over to steal her food. Intimidated, but not outdone, Poep defended her francolin as best she could by trying to slip away, but Boycat viciously tried to bully his sister out of her prize. Snarling aggressively, Poep stood her ground, facing her bigger brother who, hissing loudly, attacked her with unsheathed claws.

'*HEY!*' Hurrying towards the cubs rolling in a ball of furious fur I hovered over them like a referee in a boxing ring before resolutely dropping my hand into the battle to find a clean grip on at least one neck without getting my own fingers ripped to pieces. Again, as I had seen so often, it was amazing how, once prised apart, the cubs abandoned their hostility and resumed their close bond, initiating play and bouncing after one another as if nothing had happened. But it was the end of the shoot. Poep slunk off after a few minutes, away from her uncharacteristically grumpy brother. I tried the trip-him-up and rub-the-belly routine, but he crankily moved away and, hissing, tried to bite me, something he had never done before. But it was entirely my fault. He always warned me with a hiss or a growl when he was in a bad mood, but sometimes I wanted to test his character under pressure to see how much he'd let me get away with. Confused by his own reaction, he immediately pulled away and went off to sulk in a corner.

8
PLAYING WITH LEOPARDS

By the third week of July, with midwinter nights long and endlessly dark and the days crisp and sunny, the cubs buzzed around like live wires first thing in the morning. The chill still hanging heavily in the air, I'd open the latch and have two young leopards bolting past my legs and chasing each other around camp before Karin and I followed them on the way down to the donga. After a nice long walk we'd return to camp warmed by the soft, comforting morning sunlight after which the day grew increasingly hot. But still the cubs had enough energy to belt into my tent and jump on and off my bed, dashing across and underneath it until, finally exhausted, they slowed down to fall asleep on the confusion of trampled sheets and blankets.

Standing at the base of a robust *Combretum apiculatum* on the bank of the donga early one morning, I watched the cubs scampering after a bevy of about twenty little francolins. Scattering and flying up into nearby trees and bushes shrieking their protest, they easily escaped the two inexperienced leopard cubs. Still, I actively encouraged the cubs to stalk small prey. Boycat never tired of tearing after the taunting game birds, regardless of how many times he failed to catch them, whereas Poep often lost interest, realising they were too fast. Instead, her attention wandered to the trees which she climbed with increasing agility and strength, often staying aloft for hours on end. Sometimes when Boycat gave up on his hunting practice he joined her to play in the highest reaches of the tree canopy. Only a few days earlier in the late afternoon, with twilight about an hour away, they were having so much fun that I decided to throw caution to the wind and join them. Heaving myself up against the bark, I got a grip on one of the lower branches of a tall red bushwillow and, clambering up into the canopy, climbed all the way to the top to look into two incredulous leopard faces staring at me as if this was the last place they'd ever expected to find me. But, quickly adapting to this new development, they seemed to quite enjoy having me up there. Boycat took full advantage of the opportunity to mess with my feet, knowing I didn't have as good a grip as he did, while Poep gave me a few gentle bats with her paw.

Another favourite place to play games was the weeping wattle beside my tent. Silently enduring the weight of the cubs romping around on its nude winter arms, the branches shuddered beneath their crashing movements while I kept an eye on them as I did muscle-strengthening exercises on the gym bench in front of my tent. I tried to do daily work-outs while the cubs were resting because it was important I remain as strong and fit as possible to keep up with them as they grew bigger and more powerful. From the tree, the canvas roof of my tent was just one short leap of faith away and, leaving the tree limbs bouncing like a trampoline, Boycat and Poepface landed on the roof with two thuds to continue their boisterous play without so much as a pause. But there were times when the cubs went too quiet for my liking and I'd stop exercising only to see two scrunched-up little leopard faces peering down at me from the top of the tent with quizzical expressions on their faces as if wondering on earth what I was doing.

One morning, towards the end of the month, I was walking behind the cubs in the direction of the donga when Boycat suddenly decided to change course, veering off to the left in front of the fireplace and around to the front of Karin's tent. Padding around curiously, he paused after rounding the canvas corner of her tent to find a washstand blocking his way. After looking up and down the crossed metal legs, his eyes came to rest at the top which supported a large green plastic basin and a bright orange enamel mug. Intrigued, Boycat circled the stand, sniffing at each of the four metal legs before marching on towards a rather fat tree stump. Scrutinising the up-turned wooden log in great detail he was scarcely aware of his sister brushing past him to investigate the inside of the tent.

Standing nearby, Karin and I watched Boycat as he nosed over a toothbrush and tube of toothpaste lying on top of the stump before moving on to a bar of soap. To our surprise, the scent of the soap didn't seem to put him off in the least. Instead, his senses clearly piqued, Boycat ran his nostrils over the bar of soap as if appreciating an expensive cigar and then, pulling it off the stump with his paw, he tried to clutch it to his chest and brushed his chin over it with long sideways strokes, left and right, right and left, savouring the experience and oblivious to our giggling.

I knew these moments would become treasured memories in time to come. I'd taken on the responsibility of looking after the cubs in the full knowledge that our time together would be limited. A year perhaps. Maybe slightly longer. But after that Boycat and Poep would be young adult leopards and ready to be released in a wild area where they would pursue the life they were supposed to live and where any chances of my ever seeing them again would be slight, if not totally non-existent. I hadn't wanted to dwell too much on this, knowing it would probably break my heart to have to say goodbye, but I did want to make sure that I'd be able to relive every last minute of the time I'd spent with them and, for this reason, I recorded the cubs' progress in a black A4-size lined notebook every evening before going to sleep.

With the lamp spluttering and choking on the last remnant of paraffin I opened the notebook and, paging to the last entry, I started to write.

26 July. Had breakfast with Jimmy at Main Camp yesterday morning, called Cha and then drove back to camp to let the kids out. After almost two months they are beginning to change. Their fur feels different. It's much coarser and their spot pattern is showing more definition. Longer guard hairs have appeared on their backs and I first noticed the change on their legs. Boycat in particular shows that rich golden bronze sheen of an adult leopard.

Poep is taking a little longer to develop than Boycat. Her eyes changed colour about a week later than his, but both have turned brown now. Weighed and measured them yesterday with Boycat pushing the 9kg mark, whereas she is about 7kg. The pads of his front feet are 7 cm long and 5 cm wide. The back pads 6cm and 5 cm. Poep's front pads are 6 cm long and 5 cm wide, and back 5 cm long and 4 cm wide. Both cubs' upper canines are 1.3 cm long. Their muscles are really developing and both are starting to look more like proper cats. Think my babies are slowly turning into mini leopards. Love them to bits. Karin went to Main Camp last night. Ate dinner alone and straight from the pan after putting the babes back inside the enclosure; saves on washing the extra dish. Had butter beans and mushrooms, was nice. Sat by the fire for a while before going to bed. Bloody dark night but incredible to sit out alone. Felt intimate. Heard hyena nearby so kept my eyes peeled just in case, as they sneak up on you sometimes.

The following morning I sat beside the fireplace with cold, stiff fingers cradling a mug of steaming hot coffee. My nose was cold and runny and I sniffed somewhat noisily, inhaling the sweet scent of wood smoke along with the musty odour of buffalo dung that hung heavily on the morning air. Taking another swig of the strong brew and starting to warm up, I made a mental note of the different species of birds around the camp before finishing my coffee and returning the mug to the kitchen. Then I walked to the cage to let the cubs out for the day. Predictably, Boycat and Poep were delighted to begin investigating clumps of grass and undergrowth, chasing after the smallest of rustling sounds.

At fourteen weeks old, both cubs showed a more serious intent to stalk small animals around camp. The francolins enticed them more than ever and if they weren't around there was always something scurrying about the bush. Dwarf mongooses, three-striped mice, scrub hares, tree agamas and striped skinks and all sorts of insects abounded in the undergrowth, creating interesting rustles and rushes that had the cubs on the tips of their toes. Unable to resist giving chase, Boycat and Poep went after them every single time without much success.

It was a good thing that the cubs were inside the enclosure at night when Mr Gerbellini made his appearance, otherwise his life would have been short-lived. Mr Gerbellini was a bushveld gerbil who had taken up part-residence inside my tent. Technically a rodent, but more closely related to a hamster than a mouse, he had made his first appearance late one evening as I lay in bed about a week after the cubs arrived, entering through a hole in the canvas tent flap that I only discovered the following morning when I bent down to unzip it. From then on, I often heard him pop in and out during the night time hours and, stealing a look at him with the flashlight, I could have sworn there was something Italian about him. I don't know why I thought that. Perhaps it was his eyes? Big and round, they were mysteriously dark against his caramel-coloured fur and all in all he reminded me of a well-dressed, classy Italian gentleman, which was why I started calling him Mr Gerbellini. He had a cute roundish face with a shortish light-brown nose and the first time I saw him he appeared very forward and charmingly inquisitive so I just let him do his thing. I never saw him during the day but believed that he had a burrow in the grass beneath the weeping wattle tree outside my tent.

I became quite fond of him and enjoyed letting him have a wander around the tent and, because he wasn't a rat or a mouse, he never rummaged through my stuff or chewed anything or made any kind of mess. 'Ciao, Mr Gerbellini,' I used to say in an Italian accent when I heard his little feet scuttling towards the hole in the netting to disappear in the early pre-dawn light.

THE MYRIAD OF birds that lived around camp provided a great source of stimulation for the cubs. Yellow-billed hornbills and glossy starlings often hopped around the kitchen tent and fireplace looking for scraps, and grey-headed sparrows, white-browed scrub-robins, laughing doves and black-backed puffbacks were always flitting through the trees, flying from the branches to snap up a beetle or other insects from the ground.

One morning, while on our way down to the donga, Poepface detected a small movement in a patch of dry, yellow grass about ten metres ahead of us in the riverbed. She immediately froze and dropped down into a crouching position to stare intently at a small party of Natal francolins foraging in the undergrowth. With their brown speckled bodies, the birds were well adapted to blend in with their environment, but one little francolin popped its face up over the grass like a periscope and, giving itself away without having noticed the prowling cat, continued browsing the ground for food. Crawling forward with unflinching eyes, her tummy almost brushing the ground, Poep inched forward, her concentration fixed on the flock of birds and, with a lightly twitching tail, she uttered two short muffled puffs and began to stalk slowly forward. Following his sister's lead, Boycat slunk down the bank with her, the two of them prowling across the soft river sand until they could no longer contain their excitement and rushed straight in. Like lead exploding from the barrel of a shotgun, the flock burst into the air, scattering in all directions with indignant squawks and leaving the cubs staring after them, their tails flicking with disappointment and frustration.

With a soft croaky meow Poepface came back with Boycat not far behind her after their unsuccessful francolin hunt. Bending over her to praise her valiant efforts, I stroked the corner of her mouth up along her cheek again and again with the back of my hand. The cubs were far too small to catch any reasonable-sized prey, but their instinctive stalking reaction when randomly given the opportunity boded well for their future. Unlike cheetah cubs or young lions, leopards are far more instinctual predators and I was beginning to see the early signs of their survival instinct, even without a mother to show them the way. A few days later, I gave them each a guineafowl for the first time. Boycat mock-killed his bird several times before dragging it by the throat to the cover of a bush where he could feed undisturbed. Poep took her guineafowl and immediately made away with it, struggling slightly as she straddled the dead bird between her front legs in the way adult leopards move their prey to a secluded area. With each day that passed the cubs were becoming quicker in their responses to noises in the undergrowth. Even at his young age, Boycat was as fast as lightning, something that I actively encouraged through the games I invented to help improve their speed and dexterity.

If their claws had been sharp and snappy as tiny six-week-old cubs, they were now like daggers. Boycat's feet alone were almost the size of my palm. Poep had slightly smaller paws, but I had to be extremely vigilant with both of them. I had abandoned the welding gloves I'd bought in Nelspruit, even though it made sense to wear them because I didn't want anything to prevent me from being physical with them. So along with some of my clothes I ended up using the gloves as a toy to be mock-killed, chewed and shredded. But much as they liked harassing gloves, soccer balls, old T-shirts and their little stuffed animals, a lion and leopard cub, Boycat and Poepface loved my shoes more than anything else. Every day I walked through camp with two young leopards darting around my feet, lashing out and slapping at my bush slops while I said a silent prayer that I wouldn't get my ankles clawed off. After a couple of days I decided to just take them off and give them to the cubs as they obviously regarded them as far more valuable than I did. Eyes wide with excitement and expectancy, Boycat and Poep watched as I tied the slops to the end of a piece of rope and then pulled it along the ground behind me. Giving instant chase, both cubs pounced after the shoes with unabated enthusiasm. At other times, I swung the rope in low circles over the ground, enticing the cubs to jump and leap before I relented and let them have it.

But there was one game that I reserved for Boycat alone. It was something we shared until the very end, even after he had gone wild in the South Luangwa Valley in Zambia. I would take off my hat and, sitting in a crouched position, waggle it around for him to stalk and try to steal from me. Regardless of what he happened to be doing, this attracted Boycat's attention instantly. He would peer in my direction, his ears pricked and his eyes focused intently on the movement. Then, lowering himself so that his tummy was pressed close to the ground, he slowly inched his way towards me until he was within pouncing range when, like an arrow released from an archer's bow, he launched himself on to my hat with a speed that blew my mind. In the beginning this was quite a harrowing game to play, but I soon learnt that there was one flaw in Boycat's technique. Just before unleashing his charge, he raised his bum into the air, which was my cue to pull my hand out of harm's way and save myself from being ripped up. Poor Boycat. He never understood why I'd always win and, each time we played the game and he lost, he would turn and, with an irritated shake of his head, walk away in a huff.

It was up to me to remain highly alert. As I learnt to know his ways, I came to realise that he'd be waiting for exactly those moments when I wasn't paying attention to get back at me. During the early days of our games he took me completely by surprise, but now I no longer fell for the pseudo-dozy expression in his eyes, because all I had to do was take my eyes off him for a minute and that's when he'd take his revenge. It was unbelievable how he was always on the lookout, waiting for that moment when my mind wandered and I was vulnerable. In that split second of distraction, he'd be on me. He was never malicious, but he wanted to let me know that he could nab me any time he wanted. I'd heard that leopards had a reputation for turning against one seemingly without any provocation once they were over six months old, even attacking the very people who had reared them from cubhood. But I simply didn't feel that either Boycat or Poep would ever intentionally hurt me and, perhaps to test my own belief in them, I had an opportunity to play the hat game one afternoon nine months later when I saw a large leopard moving leisurely through an area of high grass in the South Luangwa Valley.

I hadn't seen the cubs for a day or two but as I watched the leopard heading in my direction from about a hundred metres away I saw that it was Boycat. He hadn't seen me yet, so I quickly dropped in the grass and followed his movements as best I could through the mass of green stalks. At just over a year old, he was a magnificent-looking leopard, robust and muscular, but in my heart he was still my little man and I felt confident that the hard-won trust and affection that had grown between us would override any instinct he'd have to kill me. I cautiously raised my head once or twice to keep track of his whereabouts, but otherwise I remained dead quiet on my hands and knees until I saw him about seven or eight metres ahead of me. Then, lifting my hand off the ground, I moved my fingers *left-right-right-left* through the grass and, instantly alert to the faint rustle, Boycat stopped walking to lock his eyes on the movement. For a minute or so there was no sound whatsoever. I knew his body would have grown taut, his eyes focused, and that he was crouching down low on the ground, slinking forward through the grass with painstaking concentration. A short moment of anxiety came over me. I knew it was him, but he didn't know he was stalking me. For him, this was not a game. Boycat was hunting for food.

My ears began to buzz and my palms felt hot and sweaty as, for a few dizzying moments, I listened to that deafening silence. Then, suddenly, I heard him coming, sprinting through the grass. I stiffened, every muscle in my body tensing involuntarily and, anticipating his pounce as though I was a defenceless mouse, I closed my eyes. I heard the swish of something jumping and flying through the air and felt his front paws land on my back between my shoulder blades before he propelled himself off me with his back feet. I got up and saw him standing a few metres away from me, his face wearing an expression of mild annoyance at the knowledge that he had been conned, but then he came over and I gave him a good rub as he lay down beside my legs.

AS I SAT by the fire that evening, I suddenly felt inexplicably uneasy. Karin had gone to Main Camp for dinner, leaving me to enjoy the quietude of the dark night by myself. I'd opened a tin and made myself a basic stew of beans and rice and, after cleaning up, I stirred the fire and sat back to watch the millions of twinkling stars. The cubs were inside the enclosure and I was resting contentedly against the green canvas of the camping chair. A short time later I saw a hyena strolling casually along the donga, but somehow I knew that wasn't the cause of my unease. It was something else, but I couldn't put my finger on it. There was no sound from the enclosure either, indicating that the cubs had already sensed the presence of a nearby predator. I peered into the darkness but saw nothing; nor were there any alarm calls foretelling the movements of a big cat on the prowl. I sat forward slightly, listening intently. A nightjar cried in the distance, but other than that I couldn't hear a thing. After sitting quietly for another ten minutes, I got up, doused the fire and went to my tent.

After coffee the next morning, I let Boycat and Poep out and, while following them through quite a wide area of the donga that was covered in knee-high grass, I saw them stop as suddenly as if they'd hit an invisible wall. As one, two little leopard faces buried themselves deep down in the grass, sniffing a particular clump very intently. Boycat was the first to raise his head and, pulling his lips back in an odd grin, displayed his first flehmen behaviour; the natural response of the Jacobson's organ to process information of olfactory chemicals deposited by another individual of their species. As I watched the cubs spend a good few minutes interpreting the scent, I was once again amazed that they were able to share with me some of the secrets of the bush. So that's what last night was all about! And the best my own instincts could do was give me a subtle warning that a leopard was padding quietly along the Inyatini riverbed last night, virtually brushing past my dimly lit shape by the fire.

A few days later, I was walking down a dirt road with the cubs exploring the southern section deeper into the reserve, when suddenly I heard the drone of a vehicle coming towards us. This was rather strange, because the guides had been given strict instructions to steer well clear of my camp when taking guests out on morning game drives. Still, I wasn't expecting anyone and if it had been JV, he would never have taken this particular road. A little curious, I decided to keep walking; in any event it was too late to look for an alternative route.

An olive-coloured game drive vehicle came purring around the corner with a young blonde woman dressed in khaki at the wheel and, seated behind her in neat rows of three, was a rather large group of guests holding binoculars and cameras. The look of surprise on the young woman's face turned to alarm when she realised that she had driven into off-limit territory and, recovering with admirable speed, she slammed on the brakes, hastily performed a sharp three-point-turn and roared down the road in the opposite direction. Boycat and Poep were unfazed, barely paying attention to the backward stares and unsuccessful attempts by the guests to sneak pictures of a half-naked man carrying a rifle with two leopard cubs walking in front of him. We were about a kilometre and a half from camp, the furthest the cubs had ever been, but they were keen to head deeper into the new territory and, allowing them to set the pace, I moved close behind them into an area of thick mixed woodland, which I knew was not far from the Londolozi boundary with another property.

A little more cautious now, I fine-tuned all my senses. It was much more difficult to spot large animals in dense bush or to anticipate a situation that might become dangerous. Animals were so well concealed in this *Combretum* woodland that you could literally stumble over a pride of lions or a herd of elephants at the very last moment. I wasn't overly worried about lions, as they are naturally fearful of humans on foot and generally move away to avoid confrontation. Since we had mostly bull elephants in our area and very few breeding herds, I felt fairly confident they didn't pose a risk either. But I was nervous about buffalo, especially of cantankerous old bulls that were prone to lose their temper at the drop of a hat. I'd been charged by an old buffalo a few years before, but had been in a vehicle that time. It was none the less bloody scary and conjured up a new-found respect for them; enough to know that I certainly didn't fancy a similar sort of experience while out in the bush on foot. Even with the 30.06 calibre rifle I'd probably stand a better chance of beating an angry buffalo to death than trying to shoot it.

The cubs had never seen a buffalo but had encountered a small group of elephants about a week earlier. We had been exploring an area in the donga about ninety to a hundred metres south-east of Karin's tent when the loud sound of breaking branches filled the air. The cubs, unsure, looked up in surprise and, since I was always keen to introduce Boycat and Poep to new things, I wanted to take this opportunity to show them these giant animals. I moved slowly forward to spot two massive bulls stripping leaves off the branches of a large knobthorn tree. Not far from them, maybe thirty metres to their east, a third bull was feeding. Noticing a small thicket of leadwood trees not far from the elephants, I tested for a favourable wind and decided to creep forward with the cubs instinctively following close behind me.

When we got to within fifteen metres, I crouched down behind the leadwoods watching the elephants reaching high into the tree canopy with their trunks and bringing copious amounts of leafy vegetation into their mouths. Slightly unnerved, Boycat and Poep watched the grey giants, their eyes large with uncertainty. Their first instinct was to retreat but they soon realised that the elephants were far too preoccupied with food to pay attention to much else. Hiding behind my back, the cubs popped their heads up on either side of my shoulders to stare at the bulls with unbridled curiosity, until a low rumbling *TRRRRRRRRRRRR* contact call sent them scurrying behind my back for cover.

It was good for them to be cautious. By now I had learnt that the cubs had a strong sense of self-preservation and I trusted them when they showed any signs of apprehension. Often I would find lion or hyena tracks in and around the camp on the mornings after Boycat and Poep had been unusually quiet during the night. There were times however when I couldn't find any reason for what had caused the cubs to be alarmed.

Early one evening in November, when the cubs were close to six months old, we were about to wrap up filming a scene with JV and the cubs by the fireplace when Poep suddenly became very agitated. Pushing her tummy low to the ground she flattened her ears against her head and hurried towards a scented thorn tree close to Karin's tent which she proceeded to climb to the very top. It was still light, but dusk was not far off and it didn't look as if she would be coming down any time soon. This was obviously not her day as earlier that morning her brother had, during some rough play, unwittingly lashed out with his claws and scratched her eye. Her eye closed up later in the afternoon and I saw pus collecting at the corner. And now this. Poor little girl!

I thought of climbing the tree and plucking her from it, but with its long claw-like thorns and thin branches I didn't stand much chance. Also, I didn't want to add to her anxiety by forcing her out of a place where she felt safe, so I asked Karin to fetch some meat from the gas fridge in the kitchen hoping I could lure her down. But Poep would not be swayed. Not even the sight of her brother being led back to the enclosure by Karin could persuade her to come down. I hurried back to my tent to fetch my thick dark-green Guernsey jumper and returned to the scented thorn to sit down at its base and wait it out.

What could possibly have startled her so, I wondered, burying my hands in the sleeves of the jumper to keep them warm. For her to prefer staying up a tree by herself rather than joining her brother inside the enclosure was very out of character. Had she seen or sensed something prowling around camp? I looked up, and talked softly to her but Poep refused to move. Half an hour passed and it grew dark and cold. It was supposed to be spring, but my legs were freezing. Karin brought me a few cups of hot steaming coffee, but the night remained unforgivably chilly. Another hour passed. Puffs of misty air escaped from my mouth as I stayed talking to her. Shortly before midnight, six long hours later, I heard a few scratchy movements from the upper branches. My little girl was finally clambering down, descending very slowly, one paw at a time until she was close enough for me to reach up and pluck her from the bark and hold her tightly to my chest. Feeling her claws curling into my jersey for traction as I held her close, I carried her back to the enclosure, talking to her all the while as she kneaded the wool of my jumper. I gently put her down on the soft sand to be reunited with Boycat who instantly bounded over to greet his sister, batting her softly on the shoulder and rubbing his body along hers.

As I left them, I wondered how on earth they'd ever cope without each other.

9

OUT ON A LIMB IN THE CONCRETE JUNGLE

Cameramen, technical operators, production assistants, set and art directors, a gaffer and his best boy, dolly and key grip people plus make-up artists and hair stylists spilled on to the reserve during the first week of August for eight intensive weeks of filming. Scuttling about busily like little beetles, some twenty-five to thirty film crew ran around the Tree House, preparing equipment, moving props and setting up lights and cameras for the first official shoot.

JV had given the crew strict instructions not to approach the leopards or initiate any physical contact with them, but no one could blame a person for stealing a secret pat on Boycat's back as he strutted in his confident Garfield style around the set. Always one to bask in attention, he was clearly enjoying the excitement. Boycat wasn't impartial to a stranger's occasional stroke, but he never paused for long, being far too busy sniffing his way across the chaos of boxes, dolly tracks, cranes, scaffolding material and other production paraphernalia. Investigating every last unfamiliar item, he nosed his way around, his smaller sister following him rather more hesitantly.

The Tree House had been completed and looked quite stunning set atop the sturdy limbs of a gigantic jackalberry tree. The large wooden main deck now had a smaller platform on one side that could be accessed by a narrow stepladder which provided a tantalising new area for the cubs to explore. With the props in place it looked more or less like a proper safari lodge, complete with rustic furniture, African ornaments, wicker chairs, comfortable hammocks and even a faded Persian rug. Being open on three sides so that filming could take place from different angles, the one reed-like wall boasted two windows.

With the swing bridge wobbling beneath their weight, the cubs investigated every nook and cranny of the Tree House, diving into cupboards and jumping on top of the hammocks in which they swung from side to side. Only once every last centimetre had been thoroughly explored did Boycat and Poep clamber on to the hessian roof which was not nearly as sturdy as the canvas roof of my tent. The cubs' combined weight was probably close to forty kilograms and the hessian began to sag considerably. Within the first day or two Boycat had managed to claw his way through the material, creating a gap that offered him an entirely new bird's-eye perspective of the people engrossed in their tasks on the main deck. Professional technicians and set directors scurried below his eyes and, inquisitive as ever, Boycat pushed his face through the hole he had created to observe and harass anyone passing by. Too busy to notice the two bulges in the material overhead, most people were completely oblivious of the little leopard face within arm's length which gave Boycat ample opportunity to single out an unsuspecting victim. His face framed by the hessian, he waited until someone was passing directly underneath. Then, pulling back quickly, he slammed his left front leg through the opening and slapped his paw squarely on the person's head.

No one failed to be touched by him, especially now he had lost his upper left canine and looked like a naughty little schoolboy. But Poep remained very wary of the increasing number of strangers around her, unmoved by the fact that the crew were really nice and everyone just wanted to say hello to her and tell her how beautiful she was.

During the time the crew were filming at the reserve, I became quite friendly with a number of people. Justin Fouché, the director of photography was a great guy with a good sense of humour. He was from Durban, where he'd worked as a lifeguard at one of the sandy beaches before branching into the very different world of movie making. Another person I really liked was Trevor Brown, the loader, who was responsible for keeping up a constant supply of tapes for the cameras. And then there was Paul Gibbons. He was the gaffer, the head electrician. Like Duncan, Paul had been at Londolozi for the last few months working on the Xingi film and we got on from the moment we met.

By early September, the crew was about halfway through the production and awaiting the arrival of the lead female actress, Brooke Shields. We knew that by the time she arrived, there would be only four more weeks to complete the entire shoot and, foreseeing an increasingly busy and intensive film schedule ahead, JV suggested I take a few days' leave. I appreciated his offer, but I had no intention of leaving the cubs and told him I didn't need a break. But he was insistent, so eventually I relented, agreeing to drive to Johannesburg for a four-day visit to my parents.

The day before I was due to leave a car trundled into camp with a couple of Shangaan guys from Main Camp in the back bearing a collection of picks and shovels. They were going to add a longish, rectangular area to the enclosure that would give the cubs a chance to lie down and look outside without being hindered by the thick thorn scrub that covered the rest of the cage. I still kept them locked in for certain periods of the day to rest and it seemed only fair to give them the choice of remaining hidden or watching the outside world. I also thought it would make things a bit easier for me in the mornings when I was about to let them out as, hesitation now a thing of the past, Boycat and Poep often bolted past my legs in their eagerness to explore, leaving me running after them to try to persuade them to follow me to the set.

Uncharacteristically, it was Boycat who appeared nervous as the workers spilled into the camp with their equipment. He cowered, hissing in fear. Then pressing his back into a half crouch, he laid his ears flat against his head and retreated all the way to the back of the enclosure. Feeling guilty, I changed my mind about keeping the cubs inside the enclosure, away from the guys working at the far end. The noise was too disturbing.

Turning to Karin, I shook my head. 'No,' I said, 'this isn't going to work. I won't have them upset. Look at Boycat – he's terrified! I'm going to let them out.'

So I asked the guys to stop digging and to stand back while I opened the door. Poep slowly pushed her face around the corner and emerged out into the open, for once apparently unperturbed by the strangers in camp. Boycat slunk out and warily hurried the short distance to my tent where he grumpily observed the workers digging up the soil and positioning the mesh in narrow trenches. After a while, he realised that what he'd initially perceived as a threat in fact offered him the chance to pull a prank and, shuffling forward cautiously, he started to investigate how best to approach the challenge.

His eyes were drawn to the waving movements of the long trouser legs and, his anxiety now forgotten, Boycat took a few deliberate steps forward until he had crept to within a metre or two from the unsuspecting workers. Sitting down on his haunches, he watched the bottom of their trousers flapping against their ankles and, completely fascinated and unable to contain himself any longer, he dashed forward leaping joyfully and batting at the material with the heavy pad of his right paw. Whatever reaction he had hoped to evoke, the guys remained calm, heeding my advice to ignore the cubs at all times. I could only guess what was going through their minds but luckily for them Boycat soon grew bored when they just kept working and instead strode around camp looking for his sister.

Letting out the cubs early the following morning for my last outing with them before I left, I was overcome by emotion. I didn't want to go. I didn't want to leave them. Always at the back of my mind was the knowledge that we had limited time together. Why steal from that? But I had given my word to JV so after our walk I reluctantly I packed a small overnight bag and, joining Richard for a cup of coffee at the fireplace, I waited for Jackson to finish his chores and Alison to put the mop and broom away in the storage tent. Then, chucking the last dregs of liquid on to the smouldering fire I had a word with Karin before saying goodbye and getting into the passenger seat for the ride to Main Camp.

It was actually quite nice to be driven around the bush for a change and, sitting back, I relaxed and allowed myself to enjoy the drive, mostly keeping quiet and only half listening to Alison and Jackson chatting in Shangaan in the back of the vehicle. But when their conversation turned to the cubs I was all ears.

'*Eish!*' Alison muttered, shaking her head from side to side good-naturedly. '*Tingwe le tsong!*' That little one! '*Ah, Ah, Ah.*' I heard her describe how Poepface had come inside the tent she had been cleaning that morning and taken off with the spaghetti mop when she thought Alison wasn't looking. Jackson joined in, relating how he had seen Poep emerging from the tent, her teeth clamped on to the fabric dreadlocks. Straddling the handle between her front legs she had walked towards the kitchen tent in order to hoist the mop up into the marula tree. He chuckled, telling Alison that he had watched her wedge the mop between the branches, leaving it there like an ornament in a Christmas tree.

Smiling, I turned to them. '*Hlanye xingwaan yehna ranza mop ra wen, xihelhaketa ra yen xwesi.*' She's a crazy little girl, Alison. She loves that mop and thinks it's hers now! Everybody laughed.

Soon we crossed the Xabene riverbed heading north towards a small herd of nyala standing in the dappled shade of a large apple-leaf tree. Stepping elegantly on little black hooves like high-heeled shoes, the small group of females were feeding on seed pods that lay scattered on the ground. To me, these dainty antelope, with their large ears, long necks, striking red-brown coats with white stripes and scattered dots on their flanks were the epitome of grace and beauty. With not much nutritious food to be found in the dry winter season, the nyala nibbled delicately on the pods, raising their heads to stare after us with dark velvety brown eyes. Twenty minutes later we pulled into the staff car park at Main Camp and after thanking Richard for the lift and waving goodbye to Jackson and Alison, I hopped out of the vehicle and went to the workshop to find Ray, the mechanic who kept the keys of my own car for me. After a brief chat, I went around to the back entrance of the main building and through to the office to collect an exit permit that had to be stamped at reception before I could leave the reserve.

Down the stairs and past the small office where Ray's wife Lesley worked in accounts, I passed another doorway leading to the reception area. After sharing a joke with the new front of house girl – Melly had left just over a month earlier – I asked her to stamp the permit before I went looking for Cha to say goodbye. Yes, Cha had taken a leap of faith by handing in her resignation at Wits University, packing her bags and leaving her family and friends to start working at Londolozi. This was great because on weekends off she could come and stay with me in camp. We were both very happy with this new arrangement, although Poep wasn't. She wasn't too sure about the other woman in my life and had walked straight over on Cha's second visit to announce herself, whereas Boycat just enjoyed having a new lady to win over. When the weekend was over and Cha had to leave to get back to work, my little Poepface was happy to see her go. I was not.

The irony of knowing that Cha would be in the bush while I was in Johannesburg did not escape me. After hugging her goodbye, I unlocked the door of my blue VW Jetta and got into the driver's seat. It always felt strange to be back in a town car but at least the engine caught at the first attempt. How long had I been driving this car? Putting the gears into first, I backtracked to the time when my father had used it as his company car. When after five years he was offered a more recent model, he was given the option to purchase it for a soft price and had done the deal on my behalf. I had been driving it ever since.

Manoeuvring the car out of the car park I pulled away from Main Camp, driving cautiously along the rutted road. It was the first time in months that I'd had a roof over my head while driving in the bush and, feeling a little claustrophobic, I rolled the window all the way down to let in some fresh air. Heading towards the western fence line, a sinking feeling came over me. This was where wildlife ended, and the human world began.

At the Kingston Gate I handed the uniformed official my exit permit and waited for him to stamp it inside the small office. With a smile and a wave, the guard lifted the boom to allow me through and, continuing on my way, I felt the tyres grind up small stones and chunks of gravel as the vehicle rolled faster along the Kruger road west towards Hazyview.

Turning south towards Nelspruit at the traffic lights, I circumnavigated the sprawling provincial town, continuing west along the N4. Although the pulp and paper factory was still some forty kilometres away, there was already a faint nauseating smell in the air. About twenty minutes later I saw the ugly towers looming on the horizon to my right, belching sulphur like a huge dragon and polluting the sky with thick, fog-like clouds. The sight and smell of the factory almost made me do a three-point turn there and then to head back to the bush.

From Waterval Onder I began the ascent of the escarpment and after driving through the darkness of a short concrete tunnel, I followed the winding road through pretty countryside to Waterval Boven and Machadodorp. Once out of the lowveld, the environment changed dramatically, flattening out into monotonous open grassland and increasing areas of agriculture.

The N4, now a much straighter road, widened into a dual carriageway after Middelburg. After crossing the Mpumalanga-Gauteng provincial border, I first passed Witbank, then Bronkhorstspruit until eventually, after almost six hundred kilometres, the first high-rise buildings of the city rose against the distant horizon shrouded in a haze of light-brown smog.

Leaving the N4 along with a surge of other vehicles, the traffic merged on the N1 like teeth on a zipper, pressing ahead and pouring into the outskirts of the city. And as I became part of it, an old, almost forgotten tightness welled up in my chest; I felt like a new and unwilling member of a chain gang, trying to resist the impossible. I clenched my hands around the steering wheel so hard that my knuckles turned white and drove in the far left lane, trying to keep a cool head when irate drivers furiously overtook other traffic and honked their horns at cars in front of them. Joburg. I was back in the city. Signs reading Sandton and Rivonia flashed by and not long afterwards, the Edenvale and Modderfontein off-ramps. I was almost there. Flicking the indicator, I left the highway to drift along the more gentle streets of suburbia.

Just after Sandringham High School I turned right and, following the road uphill in the direction of a small block of flats, I reached Viewcrest. There was the little corner shop and café where I'd bought packets of sweets as a child and my first cigarettes in my early teenage years; it still looked exactly the same. A few shops scattered here and there, all seemingly unchanged. Right again, just after the cul-de-sac at the top of the hill, I turned into Swemmer Road, rolling to a stop before the fourth house on the left, the very house my mother had brought me home to after she had given birth to me at the Marymount Hospital almost thirty years earlier. The green shrubs and moderately tall trees I'd been so fond of in my childhood still flanked the driveway. Feeling somewhat melancholy, I parked the Jetta right at the top, beside the garage and carport. Grabbing my bag from the back seat I got out and, slamming the door shut, walked up to the front door. Dogs began barking and somewhat absent-mindedly I noticed how pretty the flower beds looked; the fragrance of jasmine in the air brought back memories of picking the white flowers and sipping the wee drops of nectar from the bud.

'Hello, Pops!' I gave my father a hug when he opened the door and suddenly realised that the last time I had seen my parents was when they had driven up to visit me in the bush eight or nine months earlier. During my days off I tended to avoid Johannesburg as much as I could, opting instead to have a break at other places in the bush. I hadn't been home for more than three years and the worst thing was that even before I set foot in the doorway I knew I wouldn't be able to cope for very long.

'Graham! Good to see you, boytjie!' Closing the door behind me, my father gave me a good-natured slap on the back and led me through the hallway while the five dogs came bounding happily towards me. Behind them in the lounge, I caught a glimpse of Jhat lying on one of the couches. Of the three, she was my favourite cat. Black and petite with the most amazing deep golden eyes set elegantly in her smallish face, she must have been close to ten years old. Narrowing her gorgeous eyes into a slight squint, she stretched out her front legs as she saw me come into the room, just as she always did.

'Hello, Jhattikins!' I sat beside her and, stroking her along the corner of her mouth and cheek, I turned her on to her back to rub her tummy. Rolling into a soft contented ball of fur, she bit me playfully while holding on to my hand with her front paws. It was lovely to see her. But, good God, I thought, had her feet always been so small? Holding her tiny paws in my hand, I couldn't help comparing them with the big lumps I was used to with the cubs.

Both Mom and Dad were keen to hear my news. As we sat in the lounge with our tea I tried my best to explain how much Boycat and Poep meant to me and how different their personalities were. My parents had always respected and supported my passion for the bush and I knew they were proud of my work with the leopard cubs. Secretly, I suspected that my father felt that the fact that his son lived in the bush with two leopards elevated his own status among friends and colleagues. My mother, whose lifelong passion for all things natural – animals, plants, flowers – had clearly been passed on to me, sat on the edge of her seat and as she listened to my stories about the cubs I could see how excited she was.

Later that night I slipped beneath the duvet in my old room. It was a little after 10pm and although I was tired after the long drive, I couldn't sleep. I lay on my back for hours, staring at the ceiling with the constant drone of traffic as my background music, even though the main thoroughfare was more than a kilometre from the house. Streetlight spilled through the gap in the curtains and eventually, accepting my restless state, I folded my hands behind my head and thought of the cubs. Were they asleep inside the cardboard box? Or were they playing, romping around on the soft river sand inside the enclosure? I was in a completely different world and it didn't feel too good. I missed them. I missed my little man and his tricks and I missed my little girl with her eyes that still at times looked haunted and uncertain. As I pulled the duvet all the way over my head, I knew the next few days were going to be long.

The following afternoon I met some friends from my high school days. The Da Costa brothers lived in nearby Sunninghill and the three of us had always been very close, particularly after we supported each other through a family tragedy. Chris, a year older, was the more level-headed of the two, while Stanley was a bit of a rebel. Stan and I were the same age and had shared the same classroom, often getting up to all sorts of mischief. It was great to see him and Chris again after all these years. Over a six-pack of cold beers, we reminisced about how different life had been when we were teenagers and then caught up on what we were doing now. Although we had been firm friends for years, I found I couldn't really explain the depth of my feelings for and devotion to Boycat and Poepface.

I wanted to let them know that it was more than just being with a pair of stunning big cats; it went much deeper than that. I'd had to work hard to win their trust and to understand how their complex minds worked, yet the sense of fulfilment and completeness I felt when I was with them was overwhelming. So I didn't try to explain my feelings to Chris and Stan. Keeping the conversation light, they commented briefly on the work I was doing before steering the conversation to other things

I got home at around 4.30pm, well before dinner. My father was sitting on the couch in the lounge doing a crossword puzzle and I watched him for a while. Peering through his black-rimmed reading glasses, lost in concentration, he was tapping the pencil up and down between his teeth and humming reflectively as his mind searched for answers. I smiled. Nothing much had changed. It was good, but it was no longer my life. Exhausted, I went to bed early, but again failed to catch up on sleep. Why did I feel like a stranger in my own world? I tossed and turned, trying to shut out the noise and the light. There was no way I could last another day.

I left early the next morning, just before dawn. My mother was sad to see me go; I could see it in her eyes although she said nothing. My father hugged me, saying they would come and visit me soon. Driving down Swemmer Road, back up the hill and past the corner shop, I stopped for petrol and, heaving a huge sigh of relief, I hit the highway, at last pulling into the Londolozi car park just before lunchtime. I dropped my keys off with Ray, found Cha at reception and then went looking for someone to give me a lift back to camp.

A light breeze played across my face, carrying the scent of elephants in the air. I inhaled deeply. At last – no more traffic fumes or polluted air. My heart felt light and free when Elmon slowed down to allow a line of wildebeest to march across the road, their black hooves kicking up a cloud of dust after the lead bull galloped into a clearing, enticing his herd to follow. Was it only three days since I had seen them? I wasn't far now. Running my hand over my head and feeling the short stubble of my brand new military crew-cut hairstyle, I thought of my father who I'd asked to do the job with his special trimmers the day before. Would the cubs notice?

Poep did. Her reaction when she saw me was to hiss loudly and pull her lips into a snarl. I quickly puffed at her and, lowering myself into sitting position, began talking soothingly to her. 'It's okay, my Poepity ... It's okay, my little girl ... Look! It's me! Just with less hair.' At the sound of my voice her ears perked up and, pushing her whiskers forward, she gave me an inquisitive look, as if she needed to make really sure. Then she slowly approached me and brushed the length of her body along my bare legs.

I was home.

10
SPRING

Although filming did become fairly intense, Boycat and Poepface were never hassled. For them, the scenes in which they appeared were just part of their daily explorations although now that the cubs were older, Poep was becoming increasingly less manageable. After a while I stopped watching the cubs when they were around the crew to observe people's behaviour instead and to ensure that no one was unintentionally hurt. I didn't think Boycat or Poep would really go for anyone, but because they saw me interacting with them so nonchalantly it was understandable that others thought they might engage with the cubs in a similar way. And that was where they were oh so wrong.

'Now is not a good time,' I'd say if I saw anyone approaching Boycat and he was in one of his stroppy moods. 'Just leave him for now.'

Despite his easy-going nature, Boycat didn't like being fussed over when he was tired after a day filled with activity. You had to be able to read his signals. There were even times when he got annoyed with Karin and tried to jump on her, as did Poep. The cubs were five months old now and, with claws as sharp as a surgeon's scalpel, they were more than capable of inflicting serious injuries. Because Poep was always the one to keep her distance, I was less concerned about her causing trouble. But Boycat had random interactions with some people, which meant that the chances were higher that someone might be clawed or bitten.

One day in mid-September we were filming a scene at the Tree House. The scene involved a corrupt nature conservation official, played by actor Norman Anstey, informing JV that he could not hand raise the leopard cubs and that they had to be locked away in a cage. When I arrived on the set with Boycat and Poep, the crew were ready. Duncan and Justin were peering through their cameras, Trevor was on standby with extra film tapes and Paul Gibbons was checking the lighting conditions. I always brought meat on to the set for the cubs and to get them to walk into the scene where and when required I rubbed it on the deck between the chairs where JV and Norman were sitting. I gave Duncan a nod that everything was in place for him to start rolling. Poepface was lying underneath one of the two hammocks, watching Norman with cold, accusing eyes while Boycat was traipsing around the set by himself, sniffing new props a few metres from where the cameras were set up. I pulled out of the frame and stood back.

'And ... ACTION!' Duncan yelled.

With cameras rolling, Norman sat down in his chair and, facing JV, took off his brown floppy bush hat which he held in his hand just below the level of his knees. Unwittingly dangling it as he moved his hands around, he went through his lines. Boycat's eyes were drawn to the hat like metal to a magnet. Strolling into the scene he went straight up to Norman and struck the tantalising moving object with his paw. Of course, this was unscripted and, momentarily taken by surprise, Norman held on to his headgear while Boycat rose up on his back legs, hooking the hat with his claws and in the process catching the actor on the finger.

'*Augh! Bliksem!*' Norman blurted out, bringing his finger to his mouth while Boycat pinned his prize to the floor and started chewing the rim.

Completely ad libbed, it was perfect, adding much more relevance to this particular scene than was originally planned.

Duncan and Justin now wanted some close-ups of Boycat hanging on to the hat while Norman's character indignantly attempted to retrieve it, but Boycat had already grown bored and had gone looking for sister. Fortunately, he could always be counted on when it came to food and when I placed a piece of meat directly underneath the upturned hat he was back in a jiffy to start pawing it again, allowing for another perfect take.

Playing the part of Christine Shaye, a young film researcher who comes to Africa and ends up helping JV to keep the cubs out of the hands of wildlife traffickers, Hollywood actress Brooke Shields arrived with her mother at Londolozi during the last week of September. Expecting airs and graces, I went to meet them at JV's house one afternoon to find two incredibly nice, down to earth people. During our chat, Brooke told me she had previously worked with captive cougars and therefore had some hands-on experience with big cats, which came as a big relief to me. She was the only person, other than JV and Elmon, to be involved in quite a few scenes that involved close proximity to the cubs and I was impressed when she had the foresight not to approach Boycat and Poep or make a fuss of them, but rather let them get used to her instead.

Spring had finally arrived. The long freezing nights lost some of their iciness and early mornings had turned pleasantly mild. Daytime temperatures easily reached the mid-thirties with large fluffy clouds pulling together like a flock of woolly sheep during the late afternoons as the heat grew increasingly oppressive. After the long dry winter, the bush looked dry and brittle, the landscape stark. We needed rain.

Every day I scanned the heavens, hoping for the season's first proper downpour, but the heat continued to build unabated without the smallest hint of breaking. None the less, life appeared to take on a new sparkle with birds, sensing a time of imminent abundance, showing the signs of early courtship behaviour in and around camp. White-browed scrub robins, laughing and green-spotted doves, bearded woodpeckers and yellow-breasted apalis – all were calling for females and chasing likely mates through the tree canopies. More and more insects crawled out of the woodwork; minuscule dainty flies danced in the shafts of the early golden sunlight and at night, vocalising loudly, katydids, cicadas and crickets rubbed their wings together in an orchestra of sound. Summer, at last, was just around the corner.

Asleep in bed one night, now with only a light sheet to cover me, I awoke to the sound of swift muffled footsteps going through the sand a short distance from my tent. My eyes flashed open in an instant. I knew that a pride of lions had pulled down a zebra just across the riverbed the night before and thinking it might be the Dudley Pride moving away from the kill site deeper south into the reserve, I sat up and listened to what I thought might be lions taking a short cut through camp. But the footfalls were not lions. Rapid, much lighter and brisk, they were like those of professional boxers, dodging around the ring to avoid their opponents' punches.

Ghroooooooogggnnnnn. A low menacing growl exploded into the darkness, cutting through the night like a jagged knife.

'SHIT!' I tossed the sheet aside and catapulted out of bed, staggering unsteadily around the tent, still half asleep. Hyenas were right beside the thorn scrub walls of the cubs' enclosure and they were making the sort of noises they use to harass other predators. A sharp cackle filled the air and I shivered, but more from outrage than fear. How dare they intimidate my babies! Using the flat surface of my open hand I slapped down hard on the canvas, once, twice and again, hoping to scare the clan and send them on their way back into the night. I quickly grabbed the torch and, shining it through the window gauze, saw that they were still milling around and sniffing the enclosure, too bewitched by the smell of leopards to flee at the sound of a human voice.

Snatching the rifle from the cupboard, I leapt towards the tent opening and, holding the 30.06 in my left hand, I rapidly pulled the zipper in the flap all the way up. Under normal circumstances, the screaming sound this produced should have scared them off. But still the hyenas circled the enclosure. So I took a few steps forward and, with the barrel pointed to the stars, let off a warning shot. Finally the clan bolted and, pummelling the ground with the pads of their feet, they loped off into the bush to disappear into the night.

IT STARTED DRIZZLING a few days later. Soft, shy raindrops trickled down from a thick blanket of grey cloud gently covering the bush with a thin film of life-giving moisture. The cubs accepted the novelty of rain without much ado, diving under acacia thickets and exploring the dense vegetation for the scurrying movements of small animals, leaving me standing out in the open, slowly getting drenched.

Back at camp, after giving the cubs their breakfast, I changed into dry clothes and made my way to the carport to drive north to JV's house to pick up some papers. Manoeuvring the vehicle along Lex's Pan, I turned on to Strip Road, and then right at the top, on to the main thoroughfare that sliced horizontally through the reserve. Circumnavigating Main Camp, I turned east to drive along the southern bank of the perennial and very pretty Sand River with its tall reeds and waving date palm fronds.

A hundred metres or so before the turn-off to Tree Camp, I saw the two Dudley Males lying in an open clearing ahead of me, gnawing at the underbelly of a freshly killed buffalo cow. Easing my foot off the accelerator, I slowed down to stop at the side of the road to watch the brothers feed, their muzzles red with blood. My heart skipped a beat as I wondered which of the two lions had been standing so close to my head only a few months before as I lay sleeping in my tent. Contemplating my own skinny body and relatively poor strength compared with that of an adult buffalo, I didn't want to think how differently that scenario might have ended.

Later, sometime after midnight, I woke to the wheezing snorts of an impala sounding the alarm about six hundred metres north of camp. Perhaps the hyenas had come back to harass the cubs, I thought, but since I couldn't hear anything else, I put my head down on the pillow and went back to sleep.

Parting the tent flap to step into the new morning some hours later, I paused to stretch my arms behind my back before walking towards the kitchen tent to make coffee. The early spring air felt comfortable and the bush had taken on a fresh colour, painted with bright green by the previous day's light rain. Humming a popular song that had somehow become stuck in my head, I continued past the cubs' enclosure until my eyes were drawn to two sets of massive paw prints deeply embedded in the soft sand. Larger than my entire hand, the tracks suggested that two adult male lions had casually strolled through camp under the cover of night and, bending down to feel the footprints with the tip of my index finger, I made a quick mental calculation. Tree Camp was only about four kilometres from camp, so it was possible that the Dudleys had left the buffalo to saunter back to the rest of their pride. It was another reminder that I needed always to be vigilant and never to ignore an animal's alarm and its likely implications.

MOM AND DAD came for a few days' visit during the first week of October. After picking them up from their room at Main Camp, we drove down Strip Road and Big Dam, where we stopped to watch a small herd of waterbuck feeding amongst some small bushes close to the water's edge. I drove further south on Tortoise Road, scaling a small rise before dipping into the sandy soil of the Xabene riverbed to head west through dense riverine forest. With camp only another two kilometres away, Mom and Dad started to become excited. Being at Londolozi was a dream come true for them and, revelling in its beauty and wildness, they felt even more special to be seeing things that ordinary paying guests would never experience – they were about to meet the cubs.

Boycat and Poep were inside the enclosure for their midday snooze, tired and lethargic from the heat and a big meal. Like most people, Mom and Dad were intrigued. At almost six months old, Boycat and Poepface were a splendid sight. I warned my parents not to try to be too friendly and said that the best they could hope for was that Boycat would come over and investigate. The cubs were no longer babies; they were young leopards.

I could see that my parents were a little daunted at being so close to two leopards. Mom crouched down, while Pops remained standing as Boycat got up to investigate them before magnanimously allowing both of them to give him a short pat. Poepface stayed where she was, just watching them. We stayed inside the enclosure with the cubs for about fifteen minutes, during which time my father tried his old dog-training routine on Boycat. 'Hello!' he said, giving him another friendly, more confident pat on the flank. But he soon learnt that his authoritative tone didn't have the effect he was used to and that Boycat didn't obey commands or take orders. A bite was a more likely outcome. Boycat gave him a quick nip on the hand and, looking quite shocked, Dad decided that was enough.

About five days after my parents had gone back to Johannesburg, I was sitting around the fire with friends who'd also made the journey from town to come and see me. As we finished a supper of tinned spaghetti and a few beers one evening, one of them remarked on the absence of a single sound other than the crackle of the fire.

'True,' I said, having just noticed the eerie silence myself. Wagging my finger and pointing to the dark evening sky, I said, 'But mark my words, in twenty minutes' time there's going to be a storm like you've never seen before.' I got up. 'In fact, we'd better take all our stuff to the kitchen.'

They were dismissive and brushed me off, saying there was no way I could know that because the night air carried not even the slightest hint of a breeze. But I had felt a buzzing in my ears, as one hears the ocean long before you reach the beach or the way you can hear a distant train approaching at high speed. I knew it was the wind racing through the trees and so I gathered the dirty dishes and leftovers and carried them to the kitchen.

Leaving my friends at the fire, I called out to them, 'You'll see! Don't say I didn't warn you!'

Soon afterwards the first violent gusts of air hit camp. Dust, twigs and ash lifted and flew in all directions. Telling my friends to store their chairs in the tent, I started tugging at a 25-litre water drum in the kitchen to force it on its side and roll it out to douse the flames, taking care not to send dangerous sparks flying into the bush and setting it alight. Coughing loudly as the sooty smoke rose into the air, I had the fire out in time to fetch the Maglite and shine the beam into the darkness, illuminating the footpath as I escorted my friends across the donga to the spare tent. Once they were safely inside I made my way back to my own tent, shouldering a particular heavy pocket of wind and briefly sidestepping to check on the cubs. I knew that the thick wall of thorn scrub was sturdy enough to protect them from the worst of the weather so, with nothing else to do, I went to my tent to wait out the storm.

For the next hour and a half the storm howled like a banshee; gusts of gale force wind slapped at the tent canvas, almost knocking the cupboard to the floor. Snuggled underneath the bedcovers, I actually quite enjoyed these extreme weather conditions. I waited for the first pitter-patter of heavy raindrops to splatter against the tent roof, but fell asleep a short while later, unaware that the storm blew over without spilling any rain.

By mid-October we still hadn't had rain. It had started to become almost unbearably hot, with temperatures easily reaching the 39 degree mark during the long daylight hours. The heat remained trapped inside my tent and by nightfall it was like stepping into an oven. It was impossible to stay in the tent longer than absolutely necessary and, eager to escape at first light, I'd leave the flaps open on both sides hoping that a gentle breeze might sweep through the steaming interior.

And then, at last, a few weeks later, the heavy summer rains came drumming down from thick grey clouds. Like rubber bullets, the heavy drops beat down with fresh, invigorating force that, by morning, had washed all the dust and sand away. New, fresh bright green shoots shot up from beneath the parched soil with tender buds appearing on the red bushwillows and tamboti trees almost overnight.

Small puddles of water, kept captive by shallow depressions in the sand, offered Boycat endless hours of playtime. Pawing at the surface as if to make sure this was the same glorious stuff that poured from the water cart when someone opened the tap, he jumped straight in, splashing around like a baby in a bathtub. At night, the pools of standing water were the source of a cacophony of chimes, croaks, pops and rasps as painted reed frogs, raucous toads, snoring puddle frogs, Tremolo sand frogs, bubbling kassina and every other frog species in the neighbourhood came out in force.

The following night, once the cubs were back in their enclosure, I opened a can of spicy beans and vegetables and added them to some onions that were sizzling at the bottom of the three-legged cooking pot on the fire. Karin had gone to Main Camp to have dinner with a few of the film crew she had become friendly with and Lawrence and Andries were both on leave. It was quiet and peaceful, the only sound that of the giant eagle owl that lived in a nearby tree. I suppressed a yawn, slowly enjoyed my dinner and then took the dishes back to the kitchen.

A gentle *auuuwwww* roused me not long after I had drifted off to sleep. Lying perfectly still, I listened to the soft contact call of a lion communicating with another pride member. Although barely audible I detected the sound of numerous footfalls coming out of the bush behind my tent and then a few louder muffled scuffles that suggested that Boycat and Poep were nervously scampering inside their sleeping box. I pushed the sheet off me and got out of bed. Quickly donning a pair of shorts, I picked up the Maglite from the nightstand and, stumbling towards the flap, pulled the zipper up and stepped into the warm night air on bare feet.

Flicking the switch on, I shone the light deep into the bush behind me, sweeping the torch from side to side to catch within the beam five large lions standing tall on all fours on the periphery of the camp, their dilated pupils glowing like car headlights. The five Sparta Brothers, on their own without their three sisters and legendary mothers, were coming into camp. I'd known these five macho males since they were tiny cubs with innocent faces and round woolly ears and had watched them tumbling over one another and chewing the fluffy tail ends of their infinitely patient mothers. But now, at three and a half years, the brothers weren't quite so cute any more. Girded by near-full manes, their heads were massive and powerful and they were youthfully inquisitive. I knew this spelt trouble.

The Dudley Males were different. Their priorities included issues other than those of these sub-adults and the only reason they ever came through camp was to take a short cut on their journey elsewhere. The five Sparta Brothers were curious and would want to investigate new things with the confident arrogance of a group of recalcitrant teenagers. And yet I felt quite sure that they'd be a little twitchy in this new environment and would be spooked as long as I stood my ground. Taking a bold step forward, I started swinging my arms over my head as I yelled. 'Hey!' It had little effect. 'HEY!! HEY!!' I shouted again, raising my voice while taking another step forward. 'VOETSAK!' Two of the lions slunk backwards until they were no longer visible in the torchlight, but the other three remained where they were, their eyes unflinching and fixed directly upon me. Still feeling fairly optimistic, I decided to use the element of surprise to send them on their way.

I took a deep breath and, mustering as much force and confidence as I could, I charged towards the three stationary lions, flailing my arms and roaring like a madman. This had an instant effect. The three males turned and bounded back into the shadows. Feeling well pleased with myself, I stepped about ten or fifteen metres into the bush, but while I was congratulating myself on this achievement, it suddenly dawned on me that I was now a fair distance from the safety of camp and that close by there were five big lions that I couldn't see. Shining the torch around me in a large circle, I took a few tentative steps backwards. Almost instantly one of the lions reappeared in the spotlight, then another. Every time I took a step back, they took a few deliberate paces forward. I stopped. The lions stopped too. My mind raced for an idea and, feeling for some small stones with the bare toes of my right foot, I sank slowly to my knees to pick them up. Yelling at the top of my voice, I hurled a few feeble pebbles in their direction. '*VOETSAK!!*'

The two lions stared at me with unbridled curiosity and I read a distinct sense of mischief in their faces. *Shit,* I thought. What have I done now? Groaning at my own stupidity for unwittingly inviting them to play this game of cat and mouse, I once again stood perfectly still. Where were the other three? Had they lost interest, or were they furtively stalking me from a different direction? I quickly checked behind me with the torch. There was nothing; just empty bush. Swinging the light back on to the two males I saw they hadn't moved. Slowly I took another step backwards before stopping once more until, after what seemed like a lifetime of stopping and starting, I'd managed to come within a few metres of the tent. More confident now, I made a dash for it and shot inside the tent to yank the 30.06 calibre rifle from the wardrobe and push my bare feet hurriedly into a pair of shoes.

I was outside in a flash and, releasing the safety catch, curled my right index finger over the trigger, balancing the barrel and the torch with my left hand. Aiming for the trees, I fired a warning shot over the lions' heads. The bullet exploded into the night air with a crashing blow and, catching my breath, I waited for them to bolt into the bush. Shining the beam ahead of me, I saw the two lions sitting tight, completely unperturbed.

'I don't believe this!'

Cursing under my breath I loaded the 30.06 again and fired a second shot, but still the lions didn't flinch. Instead, a third male walked straight into the beam to join the other two. There was only one other thing to do. But first I'd have to make my way to the carport, some thirty metres away, with three lions observing my every move and two others lurking somewhere in the shadows. Very slowly, I put one foot behind me, then another and another, until I had passed the front of my tent. Then, I turned my back, and walked cautiously past the cubs' enclosure and the kitchen tent, my nerves on edge as I listened for the slightest sound that might betray their footsteps and shining the torch behind me every three or four steps. Every fibre of my body tingled at the potential danger of lions that showed no fear of me and were at a massive advantage with their impeccable night vision.

When I reached the carport, I breathed a sigh of relief. I slipped into the driver's seat of the Land Rover and with slightly trembling hands felt for the keys that were always left in the ignition. With the engine running, I quickly connected the cable of my much more powerful car spotlight and, reversing the vehicle, I manoeuvred it on to the dirt road that led to the Tree House around the back of camp.

I found the five lions a few metres behind my tent, not far from where I'd left them, lying on their backs as though they had not a care in the world. But I'd had enough. Right here, right now, I was going to send them packing once and for all. Revving the engine as hard as I could, I compressed my lips determinedly, adjusted my direction and drove straight at them.

Jumping up, the lions trotted half-heartedly into the thickets, only to flop back down again after no more than ten metres. Figuring this was at least a start, I began reversing but as soon as I did that five massive heads appeared over the bush and the lions stood up ready to pad back in the direction of camp.

'*What the hell!*' I'd never seen such insufferable arrogance in a bunch of juveniles. With a shake of my head, I let out a war cry and tore after them until they scattered in different directions. One of the males ran straight towards my tent and, pushing down on the accelerator once more, I went after him, completely forgetting about a smallish termite mound that stood in my path. I hit the compacted sand full on with a force that threw me from the vehicle and I felt myself flying through the air before landing hard on my butt. Confused and a little dazed, I realised the spotlight was dangling on the side of the vehicle, still on and hanging from the wire connecting it to the car battery it was catching flashes of one, two, three, four, five lions as it swung from side to side like a pendulum.

'Oh God,' I moaned, instantly realising how vulnerable I was now. Inquisitiveness and amusement could easily turn into something far more sinister. Scrambling to my feet, I stood up and grabbed the swinging spotlight, turning it on myself from a low angle in the hope of intimidating them with my human form.

Whether it was that or whether the lions had grown bored, I couldn't tell but, following one another in a long line of tawny fur, the five males casually moved off into the donga, leaving me shocked and exhausted. Was I crazy to go to such lengths to protect my babies? I was sure others would think so, but I didn't really care. Boycat and Poepface were of far greater importance; greater even than my own sense of self-preservation.

11
KENYA

At the beginning of November, JV stopped off at camp with the news that we would all be going to Kenya at the end of the month to film a sequence of the movie in which he would attempt to fictitiously rehabilitate Boycat and Poep in East Africa. Feeling excited, I immediately began to imagine what it would be like to walk around the open savannah landscape of the famous Masai Mara reserve with my babies, surrounded by thousands of wild animals. I'd never been to Kenya before, but had seen loads of television documentaries about its national parks and wildlife and knew this would be a unique chance to see it for myself.

Two weeks later, JV was back, driving into camp with Jimmy, Gillian and one of the Kruger Park's state veterinarians who had come to vaccinate the cubs against rabies and administer an immune and vitamin booster to ensure they were in tip-top condition to make the journey. I'd been playing soccer with the leopards for most of the morning, something which both cubs loved. Bounding after me in the donga, batting at my legs as I kicked the ball around and hoping to manipulate it away from my feet, Boycat sometimes got a bit carried away and, unconcerned about the effect his claws were having on my skin, would tackle me with all the energy he could muster. Poepity was so much cleverer; she always kept her claws sheathed after just one firm telling-off. Anticipating the vet's visit, I gave them a big breakfast to make them a bit lethargic and mellow and as I inspected the latest scratches from earlier that morning, I wondered half jokingly whether I ought to ask the veterinarian to take a look at me first.

Dressed in customary green overalls, the vet was a young, fairly chubby guy with a pleasant face and mild manners. Offering me his hand in greeting as I approached the small group of people outside the kitchen tent, he introduced himself and waited for me to escort him to the cubs' enclosure.

'They've been fed and should be pretty relaxed,' I told him as I went ahead to the cage. 'But I would suggest that we give them some time to settle once we're inside.' Appearing slightly apprehensive, the vet followed me inside, eyeing the two impressive seven-month-old leopards he was supposed to inject. I couldn't blame him for feeling slightly intimidated.

After about ten minutes, I told him to get ready. 'He'll be the easiest,' I said, pointing to Boycat. 'We might as well get him done first.'

Advising him to stand behind me and wait for my signal, I walked over to my little man to distract him by giving him a good tummy rub and a scratch along his cheeks. Then, after a few minutes, I motioned to the vet to come closer while I continued stroking his fur. Sneaking up from behind, the vet quickly knelt down beside me, pulled at a fold of skin behind Boycat's neck and plunged the needle in without another moment's hesitation.

'Great!' I said, turning around to face him. 'That went well. Now with her it's going to be a bit harder. Just stand back and I'll try to distract her.'

Poep had been quietly watching everything from a little distance away and, observing a stranger doing something to her brother, she knew instinctively that she was next when everyone started looking at her. I sat down next to her and began talking to her soothingly and stroking the silky fur on her white underbelly and chest. But Poepface was not to be conned. She gave me a quick warning bite and then moved off to lie a few metres away. Turning back to the vet and holding up my hand to warn him to stay put, I couldn't help noticing he had gone a little red in the face. I didn't like having to push Poep into anything she didn't want to do so I left her for a little while before trying again.

'That's right. That's my girl,' I cooed, feeling her muscles relax as I ran my hand along her cheeks and whiskers. Positioning myself in such a way that she wouldn't see the vet approach, I spoke softly but urgently. 'OK. You'd better come now.' I left my left hand resting on her back, knowing I would only be able to pin her down for a few seconds. 'And you'd better be quick!' Syringe at the ready, the vet quickly knelt down beside her, lifted the scruff of her neck and stuck the needle into the fold of skin. He wasted no time jumping away when the contents of the syringe had been emptied.

During the following week I made several trips to Nelspruit to apply for a new passport and to visit the clinic for my own compulsory yellow fever jab. I was amazed to be able to collect the travel document before the week was out, thanks to a very efficient civil servant.

Two days before we were due to fly, I woke up during the night to a very strange, growling sound. My first thought was that the five Sparta Males had returned, but since I didn't hear any footfalls or soft contact calls, I struggled to place the sound. With only half a moon, I couldn't see far through the window so I lay down and continued to listen to the uninterrupted grumble that sounded like a tractor. Whatever it was, it growled the whole night, robbing me of a good night's sleep, which was annoying because I had a long day ahead of me. Now that filming had more or less come to an end, Paul Gibbons, Jimmy Marshall and I were facing another day of towing the caravans back to the caravan park in White River from which JV had rented them for the film crew to stay in. Brooke Shields had gone back to Hollywood and most of the production crew had left the reserve. The few remaining crew members who would be travelling with us to East Africa to film on location in the Masai Mara were busy organising passports, getting their yellow fever injections and generally preparing to fly in a few days' time.

Up at the crack of dawn, the growling was the first thing I heard and I was seriously concerned that a badly mauled old lion had sought refuge in the camp. I cautiously stepped into the gentle morning air on high alert only to be met by a huge bull elephant snoring heavily as he leaned against a leadwood tree in a deep sleep right in front of my tent on the lip of the donga. I stared at him with my mouth open and then couldn't help laughing.

'Okay, you bastard,' I said. 'You've kept me up half the night. On your way now.' With a start, the bull woke up and shook his head and then, flapping his ears in annoyance, he trundled off indignantly to crash through a small stand of trees on the opposite bank of the donga and disappear from sight.

I dressed quickly, reluctantly leaving Karin and Lawrence to take the cubs for their morning walk and, turning the key in the Land Rover's ignition, I drove to Main Camp. With at least another few six-hour round trips ahead, I couldn't afford to waste any time. Carefully towing the caravans behind us on to the gravel road and turning right towards Hazyview, Paul and I resumed the same nonsense as the day before, joking around using two-way radios. It made the long journey a lot more pleasant. By lunchtime, we had returned from the first trip and, after a quick bite at Main Camp, we left once more, eventually coming back one final time just after dusk. The cubs were already inside the cage when I pulled into camp, but for once I didn't feel bad for having missed out on an entire day. There wasn't much to spoil my mood, knowing Kenya was only a day away.

ON THE MORNING of Tuesday 23 November, I drove along the Xabene riverbed and up Strip Road towards the Londolozi airstrip with Karin beside me in the passenger seat and Boycat and Poepface lethargically ensconced after their sedative tablet in their new, much larger travel carrier in the back of the vehicle.

Shimmering brightly in the distance like a metal mosquito, the privately chartered King Air twin-turboprop aircraft was parked at the far end of the tarred airstrip and, from the look of things, Karin and I were the last to arrive with the cubs. JV, Elmon, Jimmy, the sound guy and a few other people were busy with last-minute preparations while the pilot, clad in smart black trousers and crisp white shirt adorned by golden epaulettes, was walking around the plane inspecting the engines. He was a slightly older guy, in his fifties, and quite heavy-set with greying hair. Highly experienced with many flying hours under his belt, he radiated confidence as he showed everyone how to pack the gear so that the best use was made of the available space. I immediately felt secure.

Carrying the cubs in their travel box towards the plane, I set them down to shake hands with the pilot before finding a quiet place for Boycat and Poep behind the last row of seats where there was a small division board. Then, slipping down to sit by the window just in front of them, I watched everyone else come stumbling into the cabin heaving carry-on luggage, backpacks and camera gear. Once all the passengers were settled and strapped-in, the pilot ascended the small stairway, pulled it up by the handrail to fold it back into the door, and turned the handle to close the door. After a short safety check, he made his way to the cockpit, his shoulders stooped to avoid hitting his head against the low ceiling.

After a twenty-minute flight, we landed in Pietersburg to refuel, clear customs and file a flight plan. As we came to a standstill on the tarmac, the pilot shut down the engines, opened the door and lowered the staircase to allow a rather corpulent uniformed customs official to inspect our cargo. Heaving himself up the steps, he pushed his frame through the small doorway and pressed his nose close against the travel box, looking at the semi-sedated cubs for a fraction of a second longer than he needed to. Then, nodding that everything was in order, he presented the pilot and JV with a stack of forms to sign before he left. Since everything had been organised weeks in advance, there wasn't much of a delay and, taxiing across the runway, we took off, lifting into the sky and bound for Kenya.

Africa stretched itself thousands of feet below my eyes and, with the engines droning in my ears, I remained glued to the window pane, hoping to get a good view of the land we were flying over. I was a bit disappointed when we flew into a thick band of cloud cover shortly after take-off so I turned to check on the cubs. Curled on their sides and lying close together on a thick base of comfortable blankets, they were fine, just a little sleepy. JV was passing around drinks from a cooler box and, accepting an ice-cold beer, I sat back to enjoy myself. This was the life! In the far distance I began to notice several large gaps in the clouds and, as if on cue, the sky cleared to reveal Lake Malawi sparkling in the bright sunlight and awash with hundreds of thousands of flamingos that appeared like pink smudges on its shores. Even from such a height, it was a magnificent scene.

At about half past one, the pilot initiated the descent toward Nairobi's Jomo Kenyatta International Airport and, after making a perfect landing, taxied towards a parking place to refuel and clear Kenyan customs. I was surprised at the wave of humidity that pushed through the open door as one by one we walked down the steps to stretch our legs on the tarmac. The air felt murky and thick as soup and was not at all what I had expected so close to the equator. Another uniformed official came to inspect the leopards and other cargo and, as soon as airport taxes had been paid and documents signed, we raced down the runway one last time to take off on the last leg of our journey. More cloud build-up obscured much of Nairobi and the Great Rift Valley, but about ten minutes after flying over the escarpment small gaps began to appear in the clouds, opening up funnel-like vacuums over the landscape before clearing completely to reveal an open panorama dotted by the occasional thorn-fenced Maasai kraal.

About forty minutes later we started our descent and, catching my first glimpse of the Mara River, I saw what looked like a huge brown snake slithering across the open savannah. Rafts of wallowing hippos were lying close together, half-submerged along its muddy banks and, further in the distance, a massive herd of elephants was making its way across the grassy plains towards the water. I'd never seen a breeding herd larger than twenty or thirty individuals and was astounded to be able to count at least eighty to a hundred individuals. Small calves with wobbling trunks tottered between their mothers and aunts, keeping up with the larger adults – an amazing sight that left me close to tears. My mind drifted to the sprawling suburbs of Johannesburg and my parents; the house in Swemmer Road and their neighbours, all perfectly neat and manicured. Were we all really in the same world?

The plane turned in a wide semicircle and, lining up for the approach towards a lonely narrow airstrip in the middle of nowhere, the pilot quickly began to descend. I almost had to pinch myself; was I really here, about to set foot in one of the most spectacular wildlife areas in Africa? For a few seconds the plane's undercarriage flew low over the tar, hovering like a dragonfly over water until, with a series of gentle bounces, the wheels touched the ground and the plane sped across the dirt strip.

Through the window I recognised Warren Samuels standing beside two Land Rovers with a fair-haired man and a few Maasai tribesmen attired in their traditional bright red shukas. JV, Karin and Jimmy began fidgeting in their seats as we came to a standstill and, with the engines shut down and propellers slowing into visibility, I too unbuckled my seatbelt. After completing his final checks the pilot climbed out of his seat and made his way through the cabin to the back of the plane where he opened the door to allow the staircase to unfold slowly towards the ground. Carrying their hand luggage, everyone shuffled along the aisle and disembarked while I remained in my seat until the last person had left the plane. Only then did I get up and descend the steps to look out over the vast stretch of open land before me.

Stepping forward, Warren reached out his hand to introduce his brother Ross and, after we had shaken hands with the Maasai as well, he gave us a hand unloading luggage and camera equipment. I knew Warren quite well, having met him a few times before at Londolozi. Kenyan-born, he was a nice-looking man in his early thirties who had come to South Africa in the early 1980s to work as a game ranger at Londolozi. He left a few years before I arrived. Since then he had returned on several occasions to discuss wildlife documentary projects with JV, who had established a private film camp on the north eastern periphery of the Masai Mara National Reserve where Warren was based.

I got someone to help me carry the travel box with the still slightly lethargic cubs out of the plane and into the back of one vehicle and, taking my seat just in front of them, we pulled away from the airstrip with Ross at the wheel. The landscape was stunning with the towering hills of the Oloololo escarpment in the background, but I was shocked to see numerous carcasses lying scattered around the savannah. Explaining that these were the countless victims of the drought which had ravaged the area for several weeks, Ross turned to me with a sad smile.

'Normally we have the long rains at this time of year,' he said. 'But,' he pointed his finger at the cloudless sky, 'it has been bone dry and the animals are suffering badly.' As if to bring the point home, we passed another dead wildebeest, its dry shrunken skin stretched over its protruding ribcage. We encountered dead animals every three or four hundred metres, most of them intact. 'Too much dead meat even for the lions and hyenas,' Ross remarked. It was a grim sight.

When we reached the camp my first priority was to settle the cubs. Showing me to a specially constructed three by four metre wire cage he'd had the staff put together, Warren helped me carry the travel box inside before leaving me to join Ross, who was showing everyone to their dark-green tents. From what I had seen so far the camp was quite basic but it was very pretty, nestled against thick riverine shrub and overlooking the Mara River. It was built on tribal ground which was technically outside the reserve. And yet animals, including lions, hyenas, leopards, cheetahs and elephants, were free to roam and wander at will, which sometimes brought them into conflict with the scattered Maasai villages. In order to protect their cattle and goats, the Maasai constructed their homesteads by building a thick, virtually impenetrable acacia thorn fence around the kraal area inside the manyatta, although occasionally the odd predator did manage to sneak through during the darker hours of the night, something it often paid for with its life. Warren had no such fence around the camp; it was open on all sides. There was a long-drop toilet and a communal kitchen and he employed the Maasai from a nearby village to tend to camp chores and a chef who cooked inside an old rusty ammunition box, using it like an oven.

Boycat and Poepface didn't appear particularly fazed at the unfamiliarity of their new environment and after gingerly sniffing their way around the cage they succumbed contentedly to their weariness after the long journey and lay down to relax. I left them to join the others for a simple lunch of sandwiches and chips, after which Chris, the soundman, and I went for a walk along the rocky banks of the Mara River. Beautiful birds I had never seen before flitted in and out of shrubs and trees and I spied my first troop of colobus monkeys across the water. Climbing to the top of a ridge, Chris and I stood silently staring over the open savannah at vast numbers of Thomson's gazelle, impalas, wildebeest and zebra nudging the plain's short grass for any remaining nutrient-rich shoots. A lonely *Acacia tortillis* shimmered on the horizon in the early afternoon heat, a classic embodiment of the East African wilderness. I loved it. This was land unspoilt by the hand of men; only tribal communities scattered unobtrusively across the plains continued their traditional lifestyle in coexistence with wild animals. This, surely, was how life was meant to be.

Later that afternoon, with the cubs still resting inside the cage, Warren took a group of us on a short drive to one of the Maasai manyattas, mud and dung huts standing in a circle inside the kraal. As I followed Warren and the others it felt as if I were crossing the threshold into an ancient world. I found the Maasai women very beautiful with their colourful beaded jewellery and bright dresses. To me, they exuded the sort of simple contentment that people in the western world would strive most of their lives to attain, probably because their uncomplicated lifestyle freed them from the shackles of modern civilisation. Walking towards one of the smaller huts, I traced my finger along the outside walls. Bulging with heaviness, they were blistered and cracked by the equatorial sun. Inside it was dark and dank with the smell of musty cow dung fusing with stale wood smoke. And yet the simplicity of this raw, earthy lifestyle and the efficient use of natural materials to provide effective shelter held an almost refined sort of beauty.

Stepping back into the bright sunlight, I walked back to JV, Chris and the others who were talking to the Maasai elders about a film shoot that would take place during the following days with the cubs inside the manyatta. Standing a small distance away, I noticed a Maasai warrior, also known as a moran, whose body was covered in some very nasty scars. Curious, I decided to introduce myself and tentatively ask what had caused them. What he then told me was probably one of the most fascinating stories I had ever heard.

In broken English, he said his name was Ngodella and that one day he and his friend had been walking across the open plains when they surprised a big male lion resting in the shade of a low acacia bush. The lion had been sound asleep and hadn't seen the two morans approaching until the very last moment when they were almost on top of him. Ngodella, who was closest to the lion, saw him coming straight for him and before he was able to raise his spear the lion was on him, its claws tearing across his chest and back. His friend, horrified, none the less had the presence of mind to throw his rungu at the animal – this is a short wooden stick with a heavy round knob at one end which is a traditional weapon the Maasai carry for warfare and for hunting small animals. The heavy club hit the lion square in the face, breaking off his top right canine, and he ran off. If his friend had not shown such courage, Ngodella would certainly have faced an untimely and unexpected death. But the most bizarre part of his story came next. About a year later, the same two morans came across the very same lion under similar circumstances. This time, Ngodella's friend was the one to be attacked. Biting him on the shoulder with the half-broken canine, the lion failed to bring him down. And so Ngodella managed to fight him off and was able to repay his friend by saving his life.

As we chatted, another young Maasai approached; a tall stunning-looking man with high cheekbones and hugely stretched earlobes.

'You are a man who can walk a long distance,' he told me, pointing at my legs with his right hand. A little taken aback, I asked him what he meant. As a child l had been teased mercilessly by the other kids at school because of the skinny legs I had inherited from my father. 'You have got good legs,' he said simply. 'They will carry you a long way.' It was probably the first time anyone had said anything nice about them.

With a little time in hand before we started filming, I took the cubs on a leisurely walk along the river frontage early the following morning. Later, I eagerly accepted the invitation to join the others on an afternoon game drive to the marsh and forests that teemed with elephants and buffalo. Hippos and monster-size crocodiles abounded in the river, whereas the savannah plains offered us incredible sightings of three cheetah brothers and a pride of lions with small cubs that tumbled over their mother's back to find their way to her swollen teats. When I returned to sit with the cubs later that evening I wondered what I had ever done so right to be experiencing all this.

The following afternoon Elmon and I went down to a section of the river where a hippo had died in a fight with another bull several days earlier. It wasn't far from camp so we decided to check it out.

'You're welcome to some of the meat for the cubs if you like, Graham,' Warren said on the second morning. 'There should be plenty left for the crocs. Not sure what the cubs will make of it though.'

So, armed with a few sharp knives, Elmon and I headed off in the direction Warren had indicated and, making our way carefully down the bank, we traversed some large slippery rocks and boulders to wade across to the carcass lying half-exposed above the surface of the water. Constantly looking left and round to ensure early detection of ripples that indicated an approaching hippo or crocodile, Elmon and I set about cutting through about five centimetres of fat before we reached the red meat inside. Later, when I presented the fatty meat to the cubs they stood over the bowls sniffing curiously before starting to feed, although from the look of them it wasn't exactly their favourite thing.

A few days later, on the Saturday morning, we set off in two Land Rovers with Boycat and Poepface in their box to film a sequence of the movie with the Maasai inside the manyatta. The Maasai had gathered in a circle inside the kraal and were watching me closely as I bent down beside the box to open the door for the cubs to come out. Being potential livestock killers, it was understandably strange for them to have someone introduce two leopard cubs in the midst of the manyatta.

Looking around them for a few seconds, Boycat and Poep began a thorough investigation of the unfamiliar mud and dung terrain. There were all sorts of smells they didn't know but after a while Boycat grew confident enough to start exploring the kraal. Poepface, unhappy with the stares of the Maasai surrounding her, decided to slink out of sight and disappeared behind one of the larger huts. Not wanting her to feel unsure and displaced,

I immediately followed her but as I rounded the mud wall I saw her, her tummy low to the ground, sneaking towards a small group of goats. In no time she had reached JV, Duncan and the rest of the film crew who were standing close together setting up the shot. Focusing her eyes intently, she used them as cover, sliding slowly and deliberately past their legs. Realising she was going to go for one of the goats and was already singling out a specific individual, I dashed towards her but I was too late. She sprinted forward and, leaping on to the back of a smallish animal, held on tight as the loudly bleating goat tried to shake her off.

In an instant the Maasai were up in arms and all hell broke loose. Everyone was shouting and in the uproar I could hear JV yelling at Chris and Duncan to keep rolling tape, while all the goats began running around in blind panic. Four or five sprightly morans jumped forward with spears raised at the ready to murder my little darling. Adrenalin was pumping through my veins, obliterating all rational thought and I rushed between them and Poep who, ignoring the chaos as her instinct to kill took over, was trying to work her way around to the goat's throat. JV grabbed a sack and hurled it at her, startling her for a few seconds, during which time she let go and dropped the little goat. It hurriedly escaped, running back to its herd. But the damage had been done and the Maasai were not amused. To them this was a serious incident and JV spent a good amount of time that afternoon trying to placate them and convince them it was just an accident.

After supper that night, I went to sit with Boycat and Poep inside the cage for a while before turning in for bed. It was a beautiful clear night and, lying flat on my back with my arms folded behind my head, I listened to the wavering, high-pitched cries of a pair of jackals in the distance. The cubs were lying sprawled across my legs and a near-full moon was rising, ascending a granite sky and casting a veil of pale silvery light over the bush. I was just thinking how perfect it all was when I became aware of soft murmuring voices all around the cage. By the time I got up to leave I had to walk past a crowd of Maasai camp staff who had silently gathered to watch me lying with the leopards. Parting almost reverently to allow me to pass, I wondered what they were thinking.

WHEN WE RETURNED to the manyatta early the following morning, the cubs appeared a little nervous because of the bellowing and bleating sounds from the cows and goats that had been rounded up and kept inside the kraal for a specific shot in the film. After the incident of the previous day, I would have thought that the livestock would have been kept away. Naturally, Boycat and Poep were intrigued to find so many animals in close proximity and, naturally, they began stalking some of the younger goats. What everyone surely should have foreseen happened very quickly. Both cubs suddenly shot forward and each pounced on a goat. Boy got bucked off his almost instantly but Poepface held on tenaciously, while everyone in the kraal was screaming and shouting. Fearing that I wouldn't be able to prevent her certain fate twice in a row, I ran towards her and managed to scoop her off the ground and carry her out of harm's way, trembling under the hostile gaze of the morans who were preparing to throw their spears and rungus. No longer accepting this as another accident, the Maasai were visibly upset and summoned their tribal elders. Compensation was demanded and JV's friendly relations with the tribe were on shaky ground.

This time Boycat and Poep had gone too far.

12
NICK

It was only because of JV's diplomatic skills and years of friendship with the Maasai that the conflict was resolved and we were able to continue filming for the rest of the week. The only other incident occurred when Boycat was approached by two morans who were challenging each other to go up to him and stroke his fur. Boycat was sitting on the back of an open Land Rover and, sensing their trepidation, waited calmly until they came near enough for him to give one of them good bite on the hand. Again, my little man faced the ire of two indignant tribal warriors. Foreseeing big trouble, I managed to get between them, happily risking taking a spear or two for my lovely boy.

A few days later, as we were filming the cubs up a lone tree, a massive herd of elephants had appeared out of nowhere, making their way towards the river to drink. Always seizing the chance of a good shot, JV suggested we try to get nearer to the herd. On our stomachs, JV, Jimmy, Elmon, Karin and I, with Boycat and Poep flanking me, crawled towards a small ridge like soldiers in a trench. As JV and Jimmy filmed and we watched the elephants traipse past, I stole a glance at the cubs. They seemed a little intimidated and stayed close to my shoulders. It was another unforgettable experience that would stay with me for ever.

The ten days flew by and before I knew it we were rattling back down the road with all our gear on our way to the airstrip for the flight back to South Africa. Once there, we loaded the cubs in the back of the King Air jet and, taking our leave of Warren and Ross, we boarded the plane and strapped ourselves into our seats.

As we lifted off into a pristine blue sky, the Masai Mara slowly faded from view. I looked back at the cubs who were lying sleepily inside the travel box, again after a big breakfast and a sedative. Turning to look down at the savannah beneath me I soaked up the last minutes of the Mara until, some thirty minutes later a formation of clouds began to gather over the Great Rift Valley. I sat back with my eyes closed and wondered if I would ever return.

About forty-five minutes later we touched down at Jomo Kenyatta International, taxiing alongside monstrously big planes that were parked at the gates, and after refuelling we flew straight to South Africa.

I was curious to see how the cubs would react to being back in their old familiar haunts, but as it turned out Boycat and Poep barely reacted at all, stepping out of the travel crate as casually as if they had just come back from a film shoot in a different part of the reserve. And yet, somewhere deep inside their minds, I was sure the journey had left its mark and that they now knew there was a bigger world out there. Perhaps as a result of exploring the completely new environment of the Mara, they appeared increasingly keen to venture further from camp. This now presented me with the challenge of ensuring that Boycat and Poep followed me back before dusk when the Londolozi predators roused themselves to hunt under the cover of dark. It wasn't just that they wanted to explore for longer, but in the extremely oppressive December weather the cubs were inclined to curl up lethargically under a bush to sleep until the air began to cool.

Sometimes, when my efforts to coax them back with a titbit of meat failed,

I was forced to pick Boycat up and carry him all the way back to camp, with Poep automatically following behind, too scared to be left alone. At eight and a half months old, the cubs were now both big and heavy and Boycat resented being carried when he wanted to keep exploring. I'd found that the best way to handle him was to slip my left hand between his back legs and along his tummy towards his chest and sweep him up into the air so that the length of his thirty-kilogram body rested on my arm as if he was lying on the branch of a tree. With his bum resting against my ribcage, I'd tickle his chest with my right hand and, feeling him relax, I managed to stop him fighting against being held. At other times I'd sneak my head beneath his belly and, in one rapid movement, simply chuck him over my neck and shoulders like a fur stole.

About a week later, Karin and I had a meeting with JV. He told us that he had been talking to the Zambian authorities and was trying to obtain permission to release Xingi and the cubs in a remote part of the South Luangwa Valley.

'Xingi's almost three now,' he said, 'and we feel she is ready to go. The idea is to set up two separate camps close to the National Park; one for her and the other for you and the cubs.' He looked at both of us. 'It'll be dangerous and nothing has been confirmed, so it is not definite. But,' he added, 'I need you both to really think about this. Zambia a wild place. None of the bigger wildlife is habituated to people as it is here. There are plenty of lion, buffalo and elephants and the Luangwa River has the densest concentration of crocodiles and hippos of any other body of water in Africa. It's tough and it will be hard and extremely dangerous. And then there is the issue of malaria ...'

He kept on talking, reiterating the dangers over and over again without even once mentioning the beauty of the park or how incredible it would be to experience Zambia with the cubs.

'Well, count me in,' I blurted without thinking. It sounded like paradise to me, but JV didn't seem to appreciate my enthusiasm.

'This is not a game, Graham,' he snapped. 'This is a serious issue and I need you both to consider carefully before making a decision.'

I shut my mouth, a little taken aback by his vehemence, but I realised he was probably feeling very pressured. After all, as the man in overall charge of the entire project, he was responsible for our safety at the end of the day. And so I agreed to give it some thought first, even though in my heart I knew I needed no such time. Besides, there wasn't a person in the world who could convince me to leave my babies until the time came when they decided to leave me. And that would be hard enough.

A gale force wind struck up later that evening as I lay in bed and, knowing that a massive storm was on the way, I got up when another gust of air blew through the gauze, opened the tent and stepped out into the refreshing breeze to double-check that the guy ropes and pegs were secure. It had become unbearably hot over the past few days. Post-lunch napping was pretty much impossible as the interior of the tents were like blazing furnaces. By morning, the towel I slept on was soaking wet after absorbing a night's perspiration and as the sun rose and daytime temperatures soared, the whole cycle started all over again. The cubs, too, were battling with the gruelling heat. Unable to expend energy for more than an hour or two, they simply crashed after breakfast until the late hours of the afternoon.

I quickly checked around the tent and, zipping down the outside flaps, I went back inside and flopped back on the bed just as a plump raindrop splattered against the canvas, followed by another and another, until the night sky simply opened up to release a deluge of water which drummed down heavily on the roof. Unable to sleep, I thought about what JV had said earlier about Zambia. The South Luangwa Valley was surely one of the continent's most remote wilderness areas and the Luangwa River was one of Africa's greatest. I'd always dreamed of living in a place like that and understood the dangers. But I wasn't scared for myself; I was concerned only about what these dangers meant for the cubs.

'A higher concentration of hippos and crocodiles than any other river in Africa.' JV's voice rang in my ears and I shivered involuntarily.

Boycat. He just didn't have a natural fear of water. And I wanted him to be afraid. I needed him to be aware of its dangers instead of simply jumping into the first puddle he saw. He would play for hours, getting himself soaking wet until eventually he'd reluctantly emerge with sheets of rainwater dripping off his belly. He never even bothered to give himself a good shake. Poep, in the meantime, would stand at the edge of the puddle, uncertainly tapping the surface with her paw. Always one to have a sense of humour, Boycat often pounced on her as she stood with her back to him and pushed her in, quickly leaping away to avoid her angry swats as she emerged from the puddle hissing and growling.

I sighed. Zambia. The dangers weren't the only things on my mind. For all its excitement, Zambia's darkest shadow was that it heralded the end of my time with the cubs. Once in that wild environment they would slowly revert to the bush and I'd be expected just to walk away, leaving them in an uncertain world while I went back to mine, thousands of kilometres away. The very thought was like a dagger in my chest. I couldn't contemplate life without my little man or my Poepity, even though it would mean they could be free to live as wild leopards. Listening to the pelting rain, I turned on my side and closed my eyes tightly, hoping to shut out all further thoughts.

IT WAS CHRISTMAS Day. Camp was quiet and peaceful and for me it was just another day. Far removed from the tinsel, jingle bells, fake spruce trees and set menus, I was more than happy to be on my own. Karin had gone away for the holidays and Andries and Lawrence were both on their annual break. As it was, I couldn't think of any better Christmas presents than those waiting for me first thing in the morning, Boycat and Poepface bounding past my feet as I opened their cage. That night, after enjoying a toasted tuna sandwich which I had made over the fire, I relaxed to the calls of a pearl-spotted owl and gazed across the smouldering coals into the darkness. Glad for the faintest of breezes, I pushed the last chunk of sandwich into my mouth and took the Jaffle grill back to the kitchen before going to my tent. Lying down on my side, I picked up the notebook lying on the bedside stand and, folding it open to a new lined page, I began to write.

25 December

Heard the chinspot batis calling again early this morning ... funny because it seems that whenever I hear them it's going to be an unbelievably hot day. Was worried about Boycat for a few days for constantly eating grass and vomiting. Maybe just an unsettled stomach after scoffing his meat too fast the day before. He's eating properly again and looking like a fine young man now his adult canine has finally come through. The size difference between the milk tooth he lost is huge.

Took the cubs for an early Christmas walk in the cool shade of the donga. Boycat found himself a small puddle with just enough water to irritate his little sister. My heart swells to see them enjoying themselves so. Both cubs took to stalking and ambushing me but now have to really watch their moves as both are fast as lightning and look like Edward Scissor Hands with claws out. Narrowly saved my hand from being shredded by Boycat while playing the hat game. Your bum, Boy, your bum!!! If only he controlled his wiggling behind before launching ... Won't play this game with him much longer I think. Am probably already scarred for life. Cuts from when Boy ripped my leg playing soccer two weeks ago are healing nicely. The antibiotics finally kicked in and the infection's gone now. Small price to pay to be with my darlings.

Poepster came for a bit of a rub this morning. Her eyes are still brownish, only slight tinges of green in them now. Love the way her nose crinkles when she pushes her beautiful whiskers forward. Just melts me. Always

> gives me a bat with her paw when she has had enough. God, she is something so incredibly special. She knows how much I love her. Also gave Boy a big rubbing session. He loved it. Such a big floppy thing when he is in that mood. Later he tried mock mating his sister again and got a serious hiding from her for that. Am proud of my little girl.

Closing the black cover of the book, I yawned. This had probably been the best Christmas I had ever known.

A week later, on New Year's Eve, I was out with the cubs in the late afternoon when Poepface caught sight of a small duiker darting into the undergrowth some ten metres ahead of us. She took off immediately, bolting into the bush. But, unfortunately for her, the small antelope was too fast and disappeared, leaving her staring at the foliage, her tail twitching with annoyance. Perhaps twenty minutes or so later, my smart little girl locked eyes with a female warthog foraging in the undergrowth about twenty metres away. Again, she instantly gave chase, causing the large hog to tear along the bottom of the riverbed screaming at the top of her lungs until she cleared a low bank and vanished into thick bush.

Highly alert now and very excited, Poep began looking at the bush a little differently, viewing her environment as a well-stocked larder with plenty of different things to hunt. She flatly refused to follow me back to camp in the late afternoon and after trying every trick in the book, I eventually had no other recourse but to grab her firmly by the scruff of the neck and carry her back to camp. Boycat, tumbling eagerly alongside my legs and anticipating the fresh meat waiting for him, had no such ambitions and was far easier to bring home. I had to be careful, though, as carrying the leopards any distance was getting a bit risky. Poep, at almost nine months, had grown into a big girl with a mind of her own. If she wanted to, she'd easily be able to shred me to pieces. Karin's recent experiences had already taught her that she could no longer carry Boycat as she'd done before; he was so much larger and more powerful now. Not always able to read his moods, she sometimes wanted to pick him up when he didn't want her to, which hadn't been such a problem before when Boycat deliberately made himself go floppy so he'd be too heavy to lift. Lately, if she tried to carry him against his will, he would spin around and take a swipe at her.

A few days later, a fairly large herd of impala was drifting peacefully by just below camp when, unnerved by something, one of the herd suddenly broke into a run, spooking the rest. The cubs had been lying a few metres away from the fireplace and, having a full view of the antelope, they instantly took off, bolting after the herd in a flurry of sand and dust.

'HEY!' Caught by surprise, I stopped fixing the fence that kept the hyenas out of the kitchen tent and raced after them. 'BOYCAT! POEP! COME BACK!' Sprinting through a maze of branches and shrubs, I ran as fast as I could, trying in vain to keep up and feeling panic rising at the back of my throat.

As I dashed through the dense bush, I called and called, ducking and diving under scented thorn branches and other thorny entanglements of scrub and thickets until I felt a sharp stinging pain in my foot as if I had stepped on a piece of broken glass.

'Aaaaaaaargh!' I yelled, but I couldn't stop and kept running, scared that I'd lose the cubs. Circumnavigating the area in which I'd seen them dash, I ran in circles, closing the distance each time, and finally I found Boycat and Poep ten minutes later, tucked beneath a clump of thickets and still in stalking mode. Heaving a huge sigh of relief, I suddenly became aware of something slippery in my sandal so I sat down on the ground and lifted my foot to investigate. Wincing, I saw a pool of blood pouring from my heel and after taking off my sandal I found that a very large acacia thorn had penetrated the back of my heel, drilling about a centimetre and a half into my flesh before it had snapped off.

Once we were back at camp I went to the kitchen to get some disinfectant from the first aid kit. Thinking the thorn had been dislodged, I just cleaned the wound and, since it no longer hurt, I thought no more about it. But about two weeks later as I put my foot down on a small stone, I suddenly felt a sharp pain slicing through my heel. Realising that a piece of the thorn must have remained embedded in my heel, I fetched the white and orange-striped tin of Traxa from the trammel beside my bed and pasted a thick layer over the back of my heel. Then, covering the yellow ointment with a plaster, I waited for the thorn to be drawn out. After about ten days, the Traxa had drawn the thorn down far enough for me to try to squeeze it out of my heel. It was a sharp acacia thorn, almost two centimetres long.

Three days later we were walking in the riverbed late in the afternoon when I noticed a different, smaller herd of impalas not far ahead of us. Boycat noticed them first and dropped into a low stalking crouch. He moved forward deliberately while Poep, lying comfortably aloft the branches of a tall knobthorn, watched her brother's movements from above. The impalas remained unaware of us as they were grazing upwind, and they carried on feeding calmly on the fresh green shoots on the banks of the donga. For me, this was an excellent opportunity to monitor Boycat's hunting prowess.

Every now and then, when he thought one of the impalas was looking in his direction, Boycat stopped and sank to his haunches before rising cautiously a few seconds later to check whether his whereabouts had been detected. He slowly inched to within twenty or thirty metres of the impalas and, holding my breath, I watched him making all the right moves until an unfavourable breeze played with the air and an impala caught his scent and snorted the alarm. As if performing a carefully choreographed move, the entire herd turned their heads in Boycat's direction but, as if they knew they were being stalked by an inexperienced leopard cub, they remained standing perfectly still. Clearly uncomfortable with so many pairs of eyes focused on him, Boycat became unnerved. Realising that his cover was blown, he rose from his crouched position to feign disinterest and walked back to me with a miffed expression in his eyes.

That evening, after a refreshing sponge bath, I ran my hand over the countless scratches and small injuries on my legs and arms courtesy of the cubs' weaponry. JV had been clawed quite badly not long before and I was keenly aware that both Boycat and Poep were capable of much worse. I never had the slightest fear that either cub would intentionally hurt me but, remembering how I'd received the injuries, I knew it was up to me to make sure that an innocent game of soccer didn't end in something much more serious. I'd already suffered a bout of septicaemia after Boycat had forgotten to retract his claws during one of our play sessions. Sometimes, he'd mischievously leave his claws unsheathed, knowing that raking after the ball was a good way to win possession of it. It wasn't only that his claws were horrendously sharp but they tackled their meals of fast decaying meat in the hot sunlight and it wasn't hard to imagine what horrible stuff got into them.

An example of an innocent action turning potentially dangerous occurred a few weeks later when Poepface, trying to slap an object out of my hand, struck her right paw against my left ear and nicked a vein with her dew claw. Blood poured down the side of my face. A quick inspection with my hand revealed that there was no major damage and, curious to see what her reaction would be, I turned the injury towards Poep's mouth. Pushing her face forward she sniffed the wound gingerly for a few seconds before starting to lick it in a healing, cleansing sort of way. Touched by her sensitivity, I failed to see her brother show a similar tenderness when, the following afternoon, he bit down on the top of my head while trying to steal my cap.

My diet at the time consisted mainly of tinned food, sandwiches, pasta and occasionally some meat cooked over a hot fire, but I lacked a regular intake of fresh fruit and vegetables. My body soon began to react as one infection followed another. Feeling hectically tired, I made a second trip to Nelspruit to see a doctor for more antibiotics.

'What the hell has happened to you now?' The pleasant young doctor looked baffled. He examined my head wound before turning to his medical cabinet and reaching for a surgical needle. 'What are you doing to get these injuries?'

Not wanting to risk a barrage of questions, I rarely if ever told anyone that I was living in the bush with two young leopards, so I mumbled something about the general hazards of living in the bush. He stitched the wound and left it at that. I could only guess what was going through his mind when just two months later, in mid-March, I returned for more stitches. This time Poep had got me while she and her brother were romping on the roof of my tent. It had been a very pleasant cool morning and, as was normal when the weather was mild and drizzly, the cubs were in quite a frisky mood. Batting her paw out in play, she slapped me in the face and gouged a hole just below my lower lip. It went almost the entire way through and, letting out a yell of pain, I gave her a little clip on the bum for that.

'Keep those claws away from my face, Poepity,' I said, telling her she could slap me anywhere as long as it was below the neck. Back I went to the young doctor's surgery for five stitches plus one on the finger where Boycat had added insult to injury. Shaking his head, the doctor looked at me once he was done.

'Now,' he scolded, 'I don't want to see you back here for some time. Whatever you are doing in the bush, you'd better take better care of yourself!'

It was around the same time that Poepface almost made her first proper kill. Karin and I were walking in the riverbed north of camp late one afternoon when both cubs suddenly stopped and dropped into stalking mode, swivelling their ears and straining to pick up the direction of a noise neither Karin nor I could hear. Crouching stealthily forward, with their backs low, the cubs crept forward until Poepface suddenly took off by herself and almost flushed a baby duiker in the grass.

I heard her hit it and we rushed up to her. We found Poep pinning a desperately bleating baby to the ground with her paws. Startled by our sudden appearance, she let go, giving the tiny duiker the chance to run off. Without any hesitation, Poep was up, sprinting after it to catch it a second time. But the mother duiker was feeding nearby and had heard her offspring's cries. She looked up over the grass cover and called to her baby. Poep was caught off guard once more and released her prey to turn in our direction, a look of exhaustion on her face as mother and baby duiker fled into the undergrowth.

IN EARLY FEBRUARY, Nick Marx arrived at Londolozi. Born in the small English town of Weybridge in Surrey, Nick had been passionate about animals since he was a young boy, wild animals in particular. In 1970, when he was 19 years old he began his career at Windsor Safari Park before moving to Howletts Wild Animal Park in Kent, where he worked with and hand-raised a wide variety of big cats, including leopards, tigers, clouded leopards and even a black leopard. Two years later, when he was twenty-one years old, Nick boarded a plane to South Africa to become a ranger at Mala Mala, Londolozi's neighbouring private reserve, and it was during this time that he first met JV.

After leaving South Africa, Nick worked with 'Billy' Arjan Singh at Tiger Haven at Dudhwa in Uttar Pradesh, India, assisting him with the reintroduction into the wild of two leopardesses, before moving back to Howletts where he became Head of Carnivores. By the early 1990s, Nick was probably one of the world's leading experts on big cats. He and JV had kept in touch over the years and JV invited Nick to come and see Xingi and the cubs and to share some of his insights and advice. He would be staying for about three weeks in camp with us while making frequent visits to JV and Gillian to offer advice on Xingi.

I was alone in camp during the early hours of the afternoon when JV pulled into the carport with Nick sitting beside him in the passenger seat and, getting up to greet them, I immediately had a good feeling about him. Of medium height, he seemed calm and friendly and we were soon chatting easily as I showed him to his tent and explained the layout of the camp.

Already anticipating their afternoon outing, the cubs were sitting at the door of the cage waiting to be let out. Although they noticed the unfamiliar stranger, neither Boycat nor Poepface paid Nick any attention. Together they headed off towards the donga and, following behind, I shared some of their quirks and character traits with Nick as we trudged down the riverbank. It was warm and after exploring the bushes and shrubs for a while the cubs settled down in the dappled shade of a large leadwood. It was at this time that Nick decided to introduce himself. Approaching the two leopards slowly, he paused when Poepface jumped up and came to seek solace behind my legs. Sensitive to her wariness and not wanting to add to her apprehension, Nick made his way to Boycat. Bending over, he offered him his left hand to sniff. I wanted to warn him not to but suddenly changed my mind. I'd seen quite a few people try to become friends with Boycat only to get bitten but, since he was supposed to be the expert, I decided to wait and see what happened.

In an instant Boycat had Nick's hand in his mouth but just as he wanted to bite down he saw Nick's right hand come down over him in a menacing fist. 'Yes, little Boy,' he said gently, 'you can bite me all you like but if you do, I'm going to hit you.'

Dropping Nick's hand immediately, Boycat watched Nick relax his fist and then quickly seized his hand again. Immediately the fist came back down over his face and he let go in a repeat of the earlier scenario. This continued for a third time with the same result, until my little man grudgingly admitted defeat and walked off in a huff before settling down grumpily beside a small bush. I found the dynamics very interesting but knew that for Boycat this was far from over.

Chuckling, I wagged my finger in warning. 'You might think you've got the better of him, Nick, but I am telling you to be on your guard from now on, because he's going to find a way to get you back.'

A couple of days later we were back in the donga and I began flicking a rope with a T-shirt tied to the end in circular motions over my head, enticing Boycat to jump up and try to catch it. After a few minutes of playing this game I offered Nick the opportunity to interact with him for a bit. I explained exactly how to hold and swing the rope and, handing it over, took a few steps back to watch them. Bounding up and down as he tried to catch the ragged material, Boycat played on without hesitation, but I noticed that every time he darted past Nick's legs, he paused for the briefest of seconds to look at his calves. A while later Nick turned his back on him to say something to me and Boycat had his chance. Vindictively, he shot forward and gave Nick a good bite on the ankle before speeding off into the bush. Shocked, Nick cried out in pain and spun around like a top, only to find Boycat gone.

I howled with laughter. 'I told you he was going to get you back! Well, there you have it!' I thought it was pretty funny to see an adolescent leopard cub get the better of an expert but Nick, taken aback, was not much impressed.

During the third week of February, Nick and I were doing some exercises in front of my tent while Boycat and Poep were in the cage for their lunchtime rest. I was on my back lifting a few weights on the gym bench and Nick was hitting my punching bag when suddenly I heard a loud crashing sound about seventy metres north of camp. Almost immediately, a series of deep throaty growls and snarls filled the air. I sat up as if stung by a bee, dropped my weights and got to my feet. 'Nick! Come, quickly. Lions! They're hitting something near camp!'

I ran to the carport with Nick following close behind, jumped into the Land Rover and turned the key in the ignition, driving hurriedly along the road through the bush. Rounding a corner, we virtually stumbled over the Dudley Pride crawling all over a large zebra mare they had just brought down. The largest of the adult females didn't take kindly to our interruption and, snarling aggressively, she charged our vehicle, stopping just a few metres short of the bonnet and lashing the black tip of her tail around like a whip. The other lionesses were now settling on their bellies and starting to feed. Slowly backing up the vehicle, I noticed with some empathy that the zebra's eyes were growing dull and lifeless. The lioness, still furious, stood her ground for a few seconds before turning tail to claim her share of the carcass. I switched off the engine and Nick and I watched from a safe distance as the pride began tearing into their meal.

Another interesting daylight encounter with a predator took place soon afterwards. Early on a Sunday afternoon, I was on my way back to my tent after making a sandwich for lunch when I caught the most fleeting of movements just behind one of the scented thorn trees in the donga. I squinted into the undergrowth but saw nothing. Peering left and right, I listened for any sound of something moving in the bush. Karin had taken Nick to visit Xingi at JV's camp and would be collecting Andries from Main Camp on her way back so camp was very quiet. I was convinced something was out there, but since I could hear nothing I started doubting myself. Still, I remained rooted to the spot. A few minutes passed before the partially obscured face of a leopard appeared behind the trunk of a scented thorn tree. She was staring straight at the camp and I recognised her as one of the recently independent daughters of the Tugwaan Female. Grateful that I was able to identify every single leopard I'd ever seen at Londolozi, I was immediately in a position to assess the situation. From what I could see, she was alone, without her mother or sister, and she was calmly checking out the camp. Maybe she was drawn by the scent of the cubs, or she had seen them in the distance during the last few days. Averting my eyes to avoid a confrontational stare that might trigger an attack, I walked slowly back to my tent.

I sat down on the camp chair in front of my tent and looked back at the scented thorn tree. But she was gone. Scanning the bush for even the slightest flash of a rosetted coat I felt a bit disappointed, but I kept still, knowing she couldn't have gone far. After another five minutes or so, peeping over the ridge with her ears flat against her head, the Tugwaan daughter continued to spy on me from a distance of about twenty-five metres. Curious to see how she would react if I tried to speak to her in leopard language, I decided to chuff at her. She froze instantly and stared at me even more intently. Next, I imitated the low throaty rumble I often heard the cubs make when they were getting excited about something. In a flash, she sat up, half wanting to charge and half wanting to run away, now realising that her cover had been blown and she had been seen. She gave a low growl and shook her head in confusion, not understanding why she was looking at a human but hearing a leopard. Lowering her head and turning sideways, she slunk off and disappeared into the donga before sneaking another glance back over the rise a few metres to her right. Looking straight into my eyes, she shook her head again as if irritated. Then, looking at me one last time, she vanished into the bush.

13
LAST DAYS AT LONDOLOZI

I left Karin and Andries to camp-sit together later that evening and drove with Nick to Main Camp to meet Cha for dinner. Emerging from his tent, Nick was wearing neat long pants and a crisp clean shirt. I looked down at my ripped shorts and shirt and hoped I wouldn't run into Ronnie Mcalvey, the general manager. Every time I saw him he was on my back, complaining about the state of my clothes, regardless of how many times I explained that investing in a new outfit wasn't any use because the cubs would just rip it up in a few days. I usually took my ripped clothes to a Shangaan guy called Arnaldo, who also mended other people's clothes, but I hadn't had a chance to collect the last lot he had repaired. And, if I were honest, I really didn't care what I looked like.

A soft murmuring of conversation filled the air as we entered the boma to find Cha sitting by the fire. Seated at elegant tables set in a large semicircle around the small campfire, most of the guests were already on their main course. The atmosphere was distinctly romantic with the paraffin lamps flickering softly and the tapping of knives and forks on the white ceramic dinner plates. A few minutes after Nick and I had joined Cha by the fire, a waiter appeared bearing a tray with the drinks we had just ordered at the bar and, toasting the evening, we started chatting. Halfway during our conversation, Boyboy, dressed in smart black pants and a colourful patterned shirt, arrived with a wide-rimmed bowl containing layers of little impala kebabs in barbecue sauce, the traditional appetiser presented to guests before the Londolozi staff showed them to their tables. Boyboy was a great guy and I was pleased to see him on duty that night. Smiling broadly, he first offered the kebabs to Cha and Nick and then turned to me.

'Hello, Graham! How are you?' We shook hands and he asked briefly after the cubs before escorting us to our table. Over sizzling sirloin steaks served with crispy roast potatoes, green beans and chunks of tender butternut smothered in the best gravy I'd ever tasted in my life, I asked Nick about his experiences with tigers, lions and snow leopards, and mentally compared his insights with what I had learnt from the cubs. He was a fascinating man and as I listened to the incredible stories he had to tell, I thought how modest he was. Rounding off dinner with cheese and biscuits followed by my favourite white chocolate and honey mousse for dessert, we decided to skip coffee and head back to camp.

It was pitch black and dead quiet when we pulled into the carport and I switched off the engine; the new moon offered barely enough light to make out even the faintest of shapes. Karin and Andries were already inside their tents and the fire was nothing more than a sooty pile of ash. Always alert to the possibility that a predator might be hanging around camp, I fetched the paraffin lantern I had left in the carport and, lighting it, shone the lamp around before telling Nick and Cha it was safe to get out of the vehicle. Cha had the weekend off and had come back to stay with me in camp. She waited until I had slipped out of the front seat before following close behind me while Nick got out on the other side. We'd only taken a few steps when I heard a low moaning sound a few metres behind us in the darkness. Spinning around on my heels I drew a sharp breath when I saw the shadowy shape of a large lioness only metres away from Nick. I knew that at this distance there were only two things she would contemplate: charge towards us and attack, or turn tail and flee into the bushes. I couldn't take any chances on her charging so I flung my arms wildly into the air and leapt towards her with a loud roar.

She didn't so much as flinch and suddenly recognising Xingi, I dropped my arms feeling foolish.

'XINGI!' I admonished her. 'What are you doing here? You gave me a hell of a fright!'

With a few more soft moans she curled her back around my legs as if seeking human comfort and looking at her more closely I saw that she appeared a little nervous. Perhaps, I thought to myself, she'd had a run-in with some other lions and had lost her way. Now that she was an adult, Xingi often managed to find a way out of her enclosure and slipped out of camp to explore the bush alone at night. She was a real honey and I'd always had a soft spot for her, but I couldn't take the risk of her making regular visits to camp. If she decided to come round during the day when the cubs were out I had no doubt that her instincts to kill two young rival predators would be stronger than any of my commands.

'Nick,' I said, 'can you keep an eye on her and make sure she stays here while I fetch Andries?' He nodded and I hurriedly jogged to the storage tent to find Andries was still awake. I explained what had happened and he agreed to take Xingi halfway to JV's camp so she could make her own way back from there. A few minutes later, with the Land Rover's engine running once again and the headlights on, Andries left camp with Xingi padding eagerly behind.

Karin left early the next morning to go on a short break, leaving Nick and me to take the cubs to the donga. Following them down the bank to the sandy soil, we sat down to observe Boycat and Poep sniffing curiously at clumps of grass that evidently were loaded with a variety of olfactory messages. A feeling of unease suddenly came over me and I peered deep into the bush wondering if the little Tugwaan girl was still around. I had spotted her sticking her face above the bush on several other occasions since the afternoon I had engaged her in leopard conversation. Was this the reason Xingi had been upset? Had the two big cats unexpectedly come face to face? Was she still hanging around camp?

Taking the lead, Boycat began following what must have been a scent trail when he suddenly disappeared from view in a dense thicket. Instantly unsure, Poepface made her way over to me and tucked herself tightly behind my legs as she stared after her brother, nervous that she could no longer see him.

'Don't worry, Poepity,' I consoled her, bending down to stroke her cheek and whiskers. 'He's not that far away and well within rescue distance if he does get himself into trouble.'

I could still hear the soft rustle of Boycat's movements about twenty metres away and Nick, Poep and I slowly followed in his direction. A sharp snapping of twigs and a fast rushing sound erupted a few seconds later and we froze immediately. There were a few short furious growls but before I was able to leap to his rescue Boycat emerged from the bush, seemingly none the worse for wear, although he kept looking back over his shoulder before settling down at our feet. His fur was a little ruffled and bits of sand and fragments of leaves were clinging to his body, evidence that the Tugwaan daughter had brushed the pad of her foot across his chest and cuffed him for being so forward.

Early the following day when I went to the cage to let the cubs out for their morning walk, I found them both unusually nervous and hesitant to come out. Thinking it might be because of the little leopardess who had been hanging around camp, I decided to leave the door open so that they could come out when they wanted to. It must have been about twenty minutes later when I noticed both cubs peering around the wire fence. Moving

Boycat and Poep detecting the scent of other leopards in the lowveld

Boycat going for a dip in a pan of the Luangwa River

Poep mock attacking her brother

Poep relaxing on the roof of my tent

Poep (above) and Boycat (below) exploring the sandbanks of the Luangwa River

Sandbank wrestling in Zambia

The cubs paddling in a Lowveld rock pool

After trashing my tent – yet again

Boycat watching birds in Zambia

Bonding in Luangwa

Boycat showing his passion for water – in a very dangerous river

forward warily, they looked left and right before bolting past my legs to shoot straight up a tall jackalberry tree close to the donga while they kept looking apprehensively in a direction north-east of camp. More alert now, I heard a troop of vervet monkeys going absolutely ballistic somewhere in the same direction. Something was definitely out there.

It took considerable time and effort to persuade the cubs to clamber down from the tree and resume their more normal behaviour, although both paused intermittently to listen to something my own ears failed to detect. By about eleven o'clock, when it was time to head back to camp, neither Boycat nor Poep seemed keen to follow but, not knowing the reason for their wariness, I didn't want them to flop down somewhere in the shade of a bush when they became tired. So, gathering all my strength, I heaved Boycat off the ground and carried him back, counting on Poepface to follow.

For the rest of the morning and the early afternoon the cubs remained nervous, constantly staring towards the north. Thinking it best to leave them inside the cage for the rest of the day, I told Lawrence I was going to pick up Nick at JV's camp where he had spent most of the day with Xingi. I manoeuvred the Land Rover in a north-easterly direction and soon crossed the dry Xabene riverbed to drive along its dense vegetation of confetti bush, red spike thorn thickets and potato bush, eventually emerging in a more open area about two kilometres from camp. There I found seven male lions lying beside the half-eaten carcass of an old buffalo bull. Taken a little by surprise, I eased my foot off the accelerator and slowly pressed on past thick scented thorn bushes to get a clearer view. The two Mala Mala Males were lying on their backs, their front paws flopping over bloated stomachs stretched as tight as leather over snare drums. A few metres away were their five three-year-old sons, the Sparta sub-adult cubs that had shown up behind my tent four months earlier and who had stubbornly resisted my attempts to chase them out of camp.

The Mala Mala Males kept territory on the neighbouring reserve but moved through Londolozi from time to time. No one knew for sure whether one or both brothers had mated with the Castleton Females but after a gestation of about three months the Castletons had given birth to eight rumbustious cubs – five males and three females – within two or three days of each other. The five brothers had grown considerably in the three years since, but still lacked the luxurious adult manes of their fathers. We knew that they hadn't yet left the pride and were still living with their mothers and three sisters, which could only mean the Castleton Females and the three sub-adult daughters were somewhere nearby. No wonder my cubs hadn't wanted to go far with twelve lions nearby! Boycat and Poep must have heard the kill taking place sometime during the early hours of the morning.

When Nick and I got back to camp, I checked on the cubs and opened the enclosure, offering them the opportunity to go for a short walk in the donga. They appeared around the corner of the gate rather warily, but after only a couple of minutes they stopped and then fled back to the enclosure. So I closed the gate behind them and went down to the donga alone to gather an armful of kindling to light a fire. Leaving Nick sitting by the crackling flames, I went to the kitchen to fetch the heavy three-legged pot and a tin of baked beans along with a few slices of bread to make us an early supper. I was about halfway there when I glimpsed some shapes not far into the bush that I felt sure weren't normally there. During the months that I had lived in camp, I had come to know the area so well that anything out of the ordinary immediately stuck out, in the way that a person would notice a strange car in the road outside their house. Cautiously, I moved a little way towards them only to stop dead in my tracks. There, about thirty metres in front of me, five tawny shapes were lying in a semicircle in the bush and staring straight at me.

'Bloody hell!'

It was the audacious Sparta brothers again! I quickly scanned around to check whether they were accompanied by their fathers, mothers and three sisters, but relaxed when I saw no sign of them. Still, I wasn't in the mood for any funny business and I needed them to stay away from the cubs, so I rushed suddenly towards them, first grabbing a fistful of small stones and gravel that I hurled in their direction. Unlike our previous encounter, all five lions jumped up simultaneously and then, regaining their composure, they padded off lazily into the bush and I was able to get on with preparing supper.

WHEN NICK LEFT for the UK I felt I'd made a friend for life. In the three weeks he had stayed with me in camp he had made some incredibly sensible suggestions. On his recommendation, we built two elevated platforms in opposite corners of the cage to allow Boycat and Poep to have their separate lofted spaces to lie on. The shelves were barely up before the cubs had leapt on to them. Scolding myself for not having thought of something so basic but effective before, I watched them contentedly looking down at me. The next thing I did was go down to the donga to cut several branches off a tall *Combretum zyheri* and push these through the metal bars beneath the platforms to create little thickets where Boycat and Poep could hide if they wanted to. We watered the large bushwillow branches every few days to keep the leaves fresh and moist and replaced them when they had dried out. And, when Nick suggested simply giving Boycat his food before giving Poep hers, instead of separating them at mealtimes, I really felt quite stupid. I'd just throw the back leg of an impala on Boycat's shelf first and as he began feeding I gave Poep hers. They never again fought over meat.

A day or so after Nick had gone, JV pulled into camp with the news that the Zambian authorities had given him permission to release Xingi, Boycat and Poep in the South Luangwa Valley.

'We'll leave in about a month's time,' he told Karin and me, advising us to make sure we'd have sorted everything we needed to as soon as possible and mentioning that he was still looking for someone to run the kitchen and do the cooking. I immediately thought of Cha and suggested she might be the perfect person for the job.

JV looked at me thoughtfully. 'That could work, Graham. Do you think she'd be keen and able to handle it?'

As I answered positively I felt my head spinning. Only four weeks to go … Cha, would she want to come along to deepest, darkest Africa?

After picking her up from Main Camp the following afternoon to spend a weekend in camp I explained that JV was looking for a food and beverage manager for Zambia and held my breath as I waited for her answer. She didn't have to say anything. Her eyes, bright with excitement, said it all. I knew I was right about her the day I met her. Zambia would just have to prove it.

On 18 March, about two weeks before we were due to leave for Zambia, I gave Cha a ride back to Main Camp and collected my sister Celia who had just arrived from Johannesburg. Celia had made numerous visits over the last year but she wanted to spend some time with me and the cubs before we left for Zambia. On the evening before she left, Celia, Cha and I enjoyed one of the gorgeous dinners Londolozi regularly organised for their guests in the middle of the bush. Candlelight and a small group of staff to take care of us made it all the more special. Back at Main Camp, after the magical dining experience, Celia kissed me goodbye, and I assured her that everything would be fine. But as I got into the Land Rover I felt a lump rise in my throat when I looked back and saw her standing there, crying her eyes out.

The reality of our impending adventure only really registered when a group of Shangaan workers from Main Camp pitched up a few days later to slowly break camp. The spare tent was the first to be taken down and loaded into a ten-ton truck ready to be reassembled on the Luangwa River, followed by the spare cage and, on the last afternoon, the kitchen and my own tent. While Cha and I, along with a couple of other people, drove to Zambia with all the equipment in the ten-ton truck, Karin and Andries would stay behind to look after the cubs. Only once we had arrived in the South Luangwa Valley and the new camps had been set up would they and the cubs fly out with JV, Gillian, Jimmy and Xingi.

I made several trips to drop off the last boxes of my clothes and other personal belongings in my old room at Main Camp where I would spend the night before we left very early the next morning. In the late afternoon I drove back to camp with one or two of the guys who had been loading the truck to collect a last few items. It was a beautiful evening, heavy with warmth, and stars were twinkling overhead. Closing my eyes for a moment I inhaled the late summer air.

This was it. Cha and I were about to go on the adventure of a lifetime. Was it really happening? Rounding the bend of the road into camp, the vehicle pulled up beneath the thatch of the carport and came to a stop beside the parked Land Rover I had been using for the last year. I glanced up at the thatch roof where only five months ago Boycat and Poep had played for the first time. The memory evoked images of what the cubs had looked like then. How much smaller they had been! I recalled playing a game with Boycat who had been hiding underneath the thatch, but he kept dangling his tail over the edge and giving away his position. I had playfully grabbed his tail, giving it a gentle tug, and then pulled my hand away, quickly ducking out of sight before he could swat me. He almost caught me once, but couldn't understand where I disappeared to until he finally learnt not to leave his tail hanging over the thatch. Poepface, who had always been the better climber, eventually found her way down from the roof by cautiously negotiating the overhang and clambering down one of the supporting poles. Boycat, afraid of the distance to the ground, only found the nerve to come down when I moved the Land Rover to allow him to leap on to the bonnet.

I walked towards the cubs' cage, barely noticing the ghostly shadows of the weeping wattle in the area where my tent had been. I couldn't really think about anything except the cubs, consumed by feelings of turmoil at having to leave them for an entire week. With slightly trembling fingers I opened the cage door and, stepping inside, found Boycat and Poep lying close together grooming themselves and each other. I sat down beside them, stroking their sleek fur and telling them how much I'd miss them during the next week.

'We'll soon be together again,' I said. 'I'll see you both in the South Luangwa.' Cupping each of their faces in the palm of my hand I kissed them both gently on the forehead and nose and forced myself to leave. Turning back one last time, I saw them both looking at me, their green eyes warm with affection. Then I returned to the Land Rover for a lift back to Main Camp.

I felt a raw stabbing pain as we drove away from camp. It was the beginning of the end and more painful than I could ever have imagined. As we pulled away into the darkness I heard the familiar raspy calls of the giant eagle owl I'd been listening to for almost an entire year.

I wondered if I would ever hear it again.

14
ZAMBIA

Driving in convoy on dusty backroads through the scattering of local communities, we left Londolozi very early the following day, heading north. With darkness only just fading, the villages were quiet, revealing an early fire burning here and there and a solitary figure raising his hand in greeting as we drove past. Right at the back in an old army-green single-cab Land Rover belonging to Londolozi film productions, Cha and I rattled along the road following the three other heavily loaded vehicles and kicking up a huge train of dust and gravel. At the front, driving JV's Toyota Hi-Lux was John Knowles, an ex-Londolozi ranger who had agreed to come to Zambia as camp manager and would be responsible for radio communication, maintenance of vehicles and general bush duties. Behind him, driving the ten-ton truck, was Londolozi's driver Texon and his wife, with Elmon and Willie in their vehicle behind him. Willie Sibuya was an elderly tracker who had worked closely with Xingi and lived in the same camp as JV and Gillian. He was going to Zambia to continue looking after Xingi.

Once on tar, the vehicles in front of us quickly picked up speed. They whizzed along at about 120 kilometres an hour and Cha and I watched the distance between us and the three other vehicles growing by the second because the Land Rover refused to go any faster than 80 kilometres an hour.

In no time we were lagging far behind and, in the confusion, I managed to get us lost twice on a straight road. The cool early morning air quickly turned hot and since we had no air conditioning and could only lower the windows halfway, we felt quite uncomfortable. Bulging with all sorts of stuff – camping chairs, bedding, gas canisters, spare tyres, three-legged cast iron cooking pots and cutlery, plus all of our personal belongings – all covered by a heavy tarpaulin, our vehicle also carried two 25-litre jerry cans of fuel on either side of the doors. The Land Rover gobbled petrol faster than I could down a Coke on a warm day and we had to make several stops along the way to top her up, which delayed us even further.

Leaving Pietersburg behind us, we crossed the Tropic of Capricorn and, reaching the foot of the Soutpansberg Mountains shortly after lunchtime, we pulled into the town of Louis Trichardt where we caught up with John, Texon and his wife and Elmon and Willie. Having rested and had a bite to eat, they were keen to carry on, and getting back into their vehicles they prepared to pull out of town while Cha and I filled up with petrol and grabbed a takeaway sandwich from a nearby café. With suburbia behind us, we entered an area of gently waving grassland which gradually unfolded into expansive bushveld dotted by rocky outcrops and the first of an increasing number of burly baobab trees. A wave of excitement washed over me as I eyed the stunning landscape; some of those baobabs dated back a thousand or more years! I could barely imagine what they had witnessed over time, or for how much longer they would be there after I was gone.

It was close to nightfall when the Land Rover's headlights illuminated the first small buildings and houses on the outskirts of Musina, sixteen kilometres from the Beit Bridge border post with Zimbabwe, but as it was probably too late to cross we had agreed to spend the night in the small town and continue our journey the next morning. Pulling up in front of a modest-looking hotel called the Impala Lily, where the other three vehicles had already parked, we got out and stretched our legs while waiting for John who, according to the others, had already gone inside to enquire about the availability of accommodation. When he reappeared shortly afterwards, triumphantly dangling two sets of keys, everyone collected their personal luggage and followed him into the white building. The accommodation was basic and with only two rooms available we had no option but to share, but pretty manicured gardens made up for that and, with a little time before dinner, I sat outside by myself for a while listening to the cicadas and the last sweet notes of a small bird.

Setting off at first light after a hasty breakfast, we approached the concrete causeway that stretched across the sluggish low-level Limpopo River and connected South Africa with Zimbabwe. I looked down to see if there were any telltale ripples in the murky brown water that might betray the presence of crocodiles, but saw none. The banks of the Limpopo were lined with large stands of nyala and fever trees and, keeping an eye out for elephants browsing on the riverine trees, we trundled on to come to a halt before a large and rather gloomy looking building. Finding a space to park amongst the countless cars and crowded minibuses, we regrouped and then followed a slow-moving stream of men and women to fill out forms and start queuing at the immigration counter. It seemed to take forever. Finally, with passports stamped, we proceeded to clear customs and after a small group of uniformed officials had inspected every last item in our loaded vehicles we finally crossed into Zimbabwe.

After stopping off for a cool drink and some packets of crisps in the small border town, we drove east along a single-lane road sandwiched between areas of thickly wooded mopane that periodically revealed narrow sandy riverbeds on both sides of the tar and loads of vervet monkeys foraging busily along the edge of the road. We continued through dense mopane forest for quite some time until we finally entered a more open and gentle landscape with the occasional cluster of thatch huts dotted against the stunning canvas of the pristine African landscape.

After passing through Rundu our route took us north-east to Masvingo, close to the famous ruins of Great Zimbabwe, and on to Chivhu. We'd once again lost John Knowles, the truck and Elmon and Willie, so Cha and I simply enjoyed the drive and figured that we'd likely catch up with them in the next town. About a hundred kilometres outside Harare we hit the first of several roadblocks, all of which we passed through without a hitch. Closer to town, the roadblocks increased and just before the outskirts of the capital we were flagged down and confronted by a young guy in military uniform, who stared at me with cold piercing black eyes and demanded money. Neither Cha nor I carried much cash because John Knowles held all the money for border crossings and accommodation, and we didn't really want to give in to his aggression but, realising I could get us into a bit of a pickle, I hauled out a six-pack of Castle Lager and offered them to him. Standing clear of the Land Rover he looked left and right, then took the beers, tucked them under his arm, and allowed us to proceed.

After spending the night in Harare, we drove west to the Zambian border village of Chirundu, arriving shortly before dusk. Everyone was pretty tired after two long days of driving, so we stopped at the first guest house we found, a few kilometres outside of town. We stretched our legs once more and then followed a pathway to enter the small building where we found ourselves in a long rather dingy hallway. There was no reception area and we couldn't find anyone to speak to, so we wandered rather forlornly along the musty corridors and had a look around. I had never seen such an unkempt place; the walls were long overdue a fresh coat of paint and most of the furniture in the rooms was old and broken. What was obviously supposed to be the lounge looked more like a derelict railway house full of junk waiting to be auctioned off.

We were about to give up and leave this strange place when the innkeeper appeared, a gaunt, stooped man who looked well into his late sixties. Acknowledging us quietly and leading the way back along the creaking wooden floorboards, he reminded me of a creepy character in a horror movie where one by one the guests meet an untimely end during the night.

As far as I could tell, there were no other guests and I looked at Cha and raised my eyebrows, hoping we hadn't arrived at the hotel from hell. After opening a number of doors, one of which revealed a dormitory-style bedroom with several single beds spaced with almost military precision, the innkeeper found rooms for everyone, showing Cha and me to our double bedroom last. He handed us the key and, turning silently on his heels, he left with the door squeaking shut after him. I let out a nervous laugh and dropped our duffel bags on an old rickety chair before investigating the dull, grimy bathroom with its slippery floors. 'Oh well,' I said, 'it's a roof over our heads, I suppose.' Exhausted, I fell back on to the bed and disappeared into a massive cavity in the old foam mattress.

There was no sign of the innkeeper the following morning when I went down the hall to get something from the car. Instead, I found a young Zimbabwean man in the garage struggling to start his vehicle. He spoke perfect English and when I stopped for a brief chat, he told me that he was studying to be an English teacher. It came as a bit of a relief to know we hadn't been entirely alone in the house and, asking what was wrong with his car, he told me that he had been trying to start the engine for about half an hour but without success. I couldn't think of anything worse than being stuck in that weird place so I offered to have a look under the bonnet, thinking that he too must badly want to get away. My back ached after a terrible night on the old mattress but luckily, after a quick glance, I saw that one of the lead cables had come loose from the battery. I reconnected it and the engine purred back to life.

Once we were on the road it wasn't far to the border and this time formalities were quickly dealt with. Stretched out before us the Zambezi River sparkled in the bright early sunshine and as we crossed the bridge into Zambia I saw an augur buzzard circling high overhead.

'Look!' I said excitedly, pointing to the sky. 'There he goes!' I had never seen an augur buzzard before and had been hoping for a sighting for a number of years. Watching it for as long as I could, I wondered if it was a good omen.

At around seven-thirty that night we finally reached the suburbs of Lusaka, pulling off the Great East Road to find accommodation at the Barn Motel, not far from Lusaka's international airport. Unlike the previous night, we had delightful accommodation. After dinner and a sound night's sleep I woke to the gentle sounds of birds and when I pulled back the curtains I saw an oasis of neatly trimmed lawns, colourful flowers and leafy trees in the garden outside.

Breakfast had never tasted so good. After a hearty plate of fried eggs, sausage, hash browns and grilled tomato with whole wheat toast, we were back on the road to Chipata, leaving behind Lusaka's high-rise buildings to be met by a scene of old Africa. Surrounded by vast expanses of dry open grassland and rocky hills, we drove through thick *Brachystegia* woodland, unique to that area, interspersed with stands of the *boehmii* species known locally as Mfuti, and thick mopane. Every now and then we came across rudimentary villages of grass and mud huts, with chickens scraping the ground around them and young children tending small livestock who waved at us as we passed by. Women clad in colourful dresses busied themselves with domestic duties and every so often a handful of barterers and young artists sitting on simple carved wooden benches offered sculptures for sale on the side of the road. Stopping intermittently to chat to the locals, we found that everyone was incredibly friendly. The road soon began to deteriorate and, pressing on, the convoy stayed close together in case of vehicle problems, bumping and zigzagging around gaping potholes.

After a night in Chipata, we drove the last hundred kilometres to Mfuwe, a small market town on the Malawian border and the last settlement before the South Luangwa National Park, where we made a short stop to buy some refreshments before continuing the last leg of the journey to Tundwe Camp. Only a few kilometres out of town we arrived at the turn-off to the

South Luangwa National Park where the tar ended and we hit a narrow dirt road. Crunching up sand and dust and small stones as the tyres rolled across the track, we drove through endless flat areas broken by massive granite koppies and I felt a wave of excitement at being so close to our destination. The road, however, thick with mud after recent rains, slowed us down considerably and it took another three and a half hours to cover the relatively short distance to the Luangwa River. Finally, in the late afternoon after crawling through the last treacherous kilometres of heavy mud, we came to a standstill in front of Tundwe Lodge and I let out a sigh of relief.

The owners of Tundwe Lodge were the Patels, friends and business associates of JV who had kindly offered to put us up for the night before we started building the new camps the following day. Tundwe would also serve as our base for incoming mail and first port of call with the outside world. Entering the main A-frame thatched building, we found ourselves in a spacious lounge and bar area that led to an outside wooden deck overlooking the Luangwa River. The guest accommodation, at that stage still largely occupied by friends and family, consisted of smaller A-frame thatched units spread out along the river frontage with the most unbelievably stunning views. After being shown to our unit, Cha and I dropped off our stuff in the upstairs bedroom and decided to take a short walk along the river before darkness enveloped the Luangwa Valley.

We sat down on the banks to take in this new, unbelievably beautiful world; the Africa I had dreamt of visiting since I was a child. Hippos plunged and surfaced in the water honking and snorting noisily, and the bush looked rich and lush after the wet summer season with marula trees weighed down by plump ripe fruit the size of golf balls. I felt a rush of excitement go through me. This was an intact ecosystem, still largely untouched by the hand of man and wilder than anything I had ever seen before. Awesome in its simple mind-blowing perfection, I sensed a powerful energy. It was as if I had come to the place where God Himself had chosen to dwell and I felt completely at home.

The Luangwa River was about four hundred metres wide in front of Tundwe but narrowed considerably some twenty kilometres downstream, where it was no more than eight or nine metres across. It was there, on the other side, that we would be setting up camp for the cubs. Still separated from the South Luangwa National Park to the north and east by floodwaters from the recent rainy season, the area would remain an island until the waters receded in the dry season to expose wide sandbanks that connected it to the park's mainland and would open the way for Boycat and Poep to cross into the park.

On the southern side of the island the river was much deeper, twisting and turning and permanently separating the island from the game management area (GMA) where scatterings of local people practised subsistence farming, keeping a small number of livestock and growing crops. Other areas were set aside as hunting concessions where wild animals such as buffalo and elephant were at risk of being killed by trophy hunters.

The plan was that we would stay on the island with the cubs until such time as their explorations led them deeper into the wilderness and they had shown that they could fend for themselves. In the meantime I would be keeping an eye on them. Once Boycat and Poep were living as wild leopards we would remain on the island for another month, until the time came when the cubs no longer returned to camp. Of course, if it was up to me I would have stayed for ever.

We began unloading the truck that same afternoon so that Texon and his wife could make a start on the long journey back to Londolozi the following morning. After breakfast we said our goodbyes and John, Elmon, Willie, Cha and I began shifting some of the smaller items into one of the lodge's nine-foot polystyrene 'banana' boats and piling anything else that fitted into the back of the three vehicles. One of the staff from Tundwe started the motor and, manoeuvring the boat out away from the river bank, headed downstream towards the island with our stuff plus about fourteen young men from the outlying areas who had been employed to help set up camp. Turning back to our vehicles, Cha and I got into the Land Rover and, following Elmon, Willie and John, slowly drove towards a place where the river was narrow enough for us to cross by inflatable dinghy. A thin layer of mud covered the two-wheel track and, feeling the wheels of the Land Rover pull a little I drove cautiously, going no more than fifteen kilometres an hour. The river flowed lazily on our left as we crept along like snails after rain, trying to find as much traction as possible.

After a while the road deviated away from the river, passing through open grassland that was prettily interspersed with thick clumps of thorny bushes and, now that we were on higher, drier ground, I accelerated a little. Bumping along the track, the Land Rover suddenly started veering to one side and I instantly eased my foot off the pedal as it quickly slid out of control. '*Whhhhoooaaa!*' I attempted to compensate for its movements but, unable to prevent the Land Rover spinning, I realised with a start that the entire right hand side of the vehicle was slowly lifting off the ground. For a split second I thought we were going to roll and, my only option being to turn into that direction, I turned the steering wheel hard to stabilise the vehicle. Fortunately for us there was a shoulder as we crossed the lowest point of the dip and, sliding along, the Land Rover bumped against it, knocking us back on to four wheels. '*Ooooops!*' I grinned apologetically at Cha.

Finally, a torturous two hours later, we reached the narrowest point of the river, to the south of the island. I swept my eyes over a large flat sandbank that led to the island's southern bank on the other side of two hundred metres of fast-flowing water. It was to be the last home I'd ever share with the cubs.

Leaving our three vehicles parked in a small clearing a few metres away from the river, John opened the trailer to haul out the rubber dinghy he'd brought from Londolozi and, inflating it, he pushed the boat off the shore. With only two shovels to serve as oars, we rowed across the Luangwa River to the edge of the sandbank. Disembarking ankle-deep in the shallows, we pulled the dinghy back on to dry land and, carrying as much of our gear as possible, we began walking towards the bank of the island about fifty metres away. It was incredibly hot and when we came across a pool of shallow water we waded straight through it instead of walking around it, hoping to cool ourselves off. It wasn't far from the other end of the pool to the southern bank of the island and as we climbed up into the welcome shade of a stand of tall Natal mahogany trees, we saw that the local guys had been dropped off and were already busy piling up boxes and equipment. The banana boat had moved downstream with a second squad of workers and equipment for the setting up of Xingi's new camp.

Everyone dug in, and for the rest of the day we went back and forth to our vehicles to ferry the remaining items to the campsite. In the early afternoon, John and Willie left to help set up Xingi's camp while I joined the banana boat which was moving back upstream to collect more of our luggage from Tundwe. Just before sunset, the boat made one last trip to take the workers back to the GMA, leaving Elmon, Cha and me alone on the island for the night. We were completely exhausted and too tired to make a fire, so we simply opened a few tins of baked beans and chakalaka and ate them cold for our dinner.

We hadn't yet located the front and back flaps of the only tent that had been erected so far and, not wanting to leave the sides open, we had prioritised building walls of tins of food, beers and soft drinks to fill the gaps as far as possible before nightfall. We had no way of knowing whether there were any predators on the island, but as it turned out the biggest menace was a cloud of mosquitoes that was rising from the surface of the water. Scampering into the tent, we made ourselves as comfortable as we could with only a blanket to sleep under as the beds, mattresses and sleeping bags had not yet been unpacked. Feeling horribly hot and clammy I lay down, tired yet sleepless, and listened to snorting of the hippos in the river.

About an hour later I heard the distant calling of lions to the north-west, their bellowing roars reverberating heavily across the valley. Increasingly more awake, I could hear Cha scratching herself madly beside me. Elmon too. Droning metallically through the gaps in our makeshift walls, the mosquitoes were coming into the tent, biting every bit of exposed skin they could find. At first light we rose, feeling completely drained, both from scratching itchy bites and lack of sleep and looking at Cha I felt a wave of sympathy. She was covered in angry red bumps from head to toe, as if she had chicken pox. Drawing her to me, I gave her a hug and assured her that our top priority would be to close off the tent and find the insect repellent.

Later that morning I took Cha for a walk around the island to see if we could find the lions I had heard during the night and, traipsing along the banks, we spotted them resting on a large sandbank on the opposite side of the deeply flowing river. We watched them for a while, and when we returned to camp we found that another load of boxes had arrived. Unpacking the first few produced our mosquito nets and insect repellent. Cha was jubilant. Privately, I wondered if we would be left with enough blood to survive if we'd had to do without them for another night.

We decided to erect the kitchen tent furthest away from the river to the east of camp and put up my Meru tent beside it with the storage tent a few metres behind. A little closer to the river, Karin's new smaller tent would go next to John's and, finally, a tent reserved for Sam, a very nice Zambian guy who was due to start work the next day to carry out domestic chores similar to those Jackson had performed back at Londolozi. We also had the chance to meet Robert and Tennis later that afternoon, game guards from the Zambian wildlife department who were responsible for anti-poaching patrolling in our area. Tennis was the older of the two men and was pensive and reserved, whereas Robert had a certain youthful brazenness about him. He would often shock us during the following weeks by jumping into deep water to push the boat if we got stuck on one of the sandbanks, seemingly unconcerned about lurking crocodiles.

Shortly before dusk the camp began to take shape. Three more tents were up and we now had a well that provided us with drinking water. The guys from the work squad had been working at it for as many hours as it had taken me to find the components of the spare cage, which had been dismantled so that it would fit into the truck. By the time I had unearthed all the carefully labelled sides and reassembled the cage, save for a few gaps that still needed fixing, I found a perfectly circular well dug by a handful of men and their spades. I couldn't believe my eyes. It was as if someone had brought in a cylinder and cored the earth like an apple.

Staring at it, I turned to the head guy. 'How on earth did you do that?'

'Eee, Bwana …' he replied, folding his hands together in a gesture of respect, 'we just used our initiative.'

After a simple meal of tinned spaghetti and meatballs, Cha and I walked across the sandbank south of camp to one of its ankle-deep pools where we bathed against the backdrop of a golden sunset before gratefully heading for bed shortly after nightfall. Elmon took to his own tent, and all of us were glad to have some privacy. Cha and I zipped down the front and back canvas flaps, now properly secured to the roof and walls, and revelled in the luxury compared to what we had experienced the night before! Sinking down on the firm mattress with the mosquito net draped around us and insect repellent liberally applied, we felt as if we had checked into a five-star hotel.

By lunchtime the following day camp was up, apart from the last few boxes that we relegated to the storage room to be unpacked at a later stage. John Knowles had come back from Xingi's new camp after helping Willie settle in and Elmon had left to join Willie. All that remained to be done before we could relax in our new home was to deliver some small items meant for Xingi's camp that had been mistakenly left behind. Offering to make the journey downstream, I asked John to row me across the river. Then I got into the Land Rover and began to negotiate the muddy track. Fat splashes spattered all over the vehicle when I reached a particularly bad section and as I felt the vehicle struggling through the porridge-like mud I realised the tyres were fighting hard to continue moving. One last rev on the accelerator and I was hopelessly stuck.

'GRRRREAT!' I spat, already knowing that without a winch and suitable vegetation to push beneath the tyres it was completely futile for me to try to dig the Land Rover out.

The only thing for it was to walk back to the river and take my chances wading across to get help at camp. Trudging through the bush for about fifteen minutes I came to a shallow drainage line across which was an area of short open grassland with a few scattered thickets and much longer grass thirty metres or so ahead. And that's when I saw him. Over the top of the tall grass a large buffalo bull stood with muscles bunched and nostrils flaring. He was looking straight at me.

'Oh God,' I groaned. 'This can't be happening!' If there was one thing I was scared of it was a cantankerous old buffalo bull, especially here in the GMA where some of the bigger animals had narrowly escaped a hunter's bullet and were extremely aggressive.

I stood dead still, averting my eyes so as not to look him in the eye, yet somehow monitoring his every movement. I was just wondering if the distance between us was too short for him to charge and whether he would decide to avoid confrontation when he came for me, barrelling his massive body across the open grassland in my direction.

'Holy shhiiitttt!' In a state of near panic I looked for something, anything, to hide behind. There was a tall termite mound close by and I started running. I literally dived behind the mound and, closing my eyes, hugged the sandy lump with both arms to prepare myself for the bull's impact. The

earth trembled, and with a pounding heart I heard him thunder past me to disappear into the thickets. Unable to move for several terrified minutes, I eventually managed to carry on walking although my heart continued to race.

I reached the Luangwa River bank about twenty minutes later and, finding myself hopelessly alone, I was seriously contemplating wading across the deep, fast-flowing water when I heard the faint purring of the banana boat coming upstream from Xingi's camp. Suddenly optimistic, I waved at Robert and gladly accepted a lift to Tundwe Lodge to look for someone to help me dig the Land Rover out. Relating my close shave with the buffalo, I was now able to laugh it off. 'The bastard might as well have had red eyes!' I told him and the rest of the workers.

A few kilometres upriver, we suddenly came to an abrupt halt when the boat hit a hidden sandbank. This was the first of many times that I saw Robert simply take off his shoes and roll up his trouser legs to plunge into the crocodile-infested water to try to push the boat back into river. He had almost got us free when a huge hippo surfaced from a shallow channel close to the river bank and it seemed to me that it wanted to move into deeper water. I warned Robert, who gave the boat a hefty last shove and, pushing it free, he climbed back on with incredible agility.

I watched the hippo nervously as it was obvious even to the untrained eye that it was becoming increasingly frustrated with the boat blocking its path. Robert pulled the string and just as we started motoring along I saw the hippo take a massive dive beneath the surface. 'GO, GO, GO!' I shouted, expecting the huge animal to tip us all into the water at any second. Everyone started screaming. I instinctively grabbed Robert's AK rifle and, dislodging the safety catch in record time, let off a warning shot over the hippo's head as it exploded from the water beside the stern. Again it dived, once more disappearing beneath the boat. Holding my breath, I felt a dead weight drop off me when it surfaced about twenty metres to our right. My God, I thought, I knew this place was wild, but to almost die twice in one day …

Were the cubs really ready for this?

15
THE CUBS ARRIVE IN ZAMBIA

I was still fixing the last gaps in the cage when I heard the Bell Jet Ranger helicopter approaching the island and, immediately getting to my feet, I left the cage door ajar and ran down the narrow game trail to find that the aircraft had alighted on a sandbank east of camp. Its rotors still spinning, a whirlwind of sand, dust and bits of vegetation spiralled up into the air. Narrowing my eyes against the tiny flying particles I saw Jimmy carrying a heavily sedated Boycat well away from the aircraft to lay him down gently on the ground. The Zambian squad, on seeing a leopard awake enough to start rolling his head from side to side, turned on their heels and fled. Hurrying forward, I saw Karin bearing heavy luggage in the direction of the tents and Anthony Bannister, the wildlife photographer, who was out of the helicopter and snapping away at the cubs with his camera.

Rushing over, I knelt beside Jimmy to check on a very groggy Boycat before getting up to see if Poep was all right in the back of the aircraft.

'She's quite alert, Graham ...' Jimmy called over the noise of the whirring metal blades as I made my way to the chopper's open back door shielding my face and hunching my shoulders against the gusts of piercing sand. Rob Parsons, the pilot, was still sitting behind the instruments ready for a speedy lift-off and another trip to Mfuwe airport to fetch JV, Gillian and Xingi. Pushing my head inside the chopper's back door, I saw Poepface lying limply on a canvas sheet. Her claws were out and her eyes were hugely dilated, and although she was slightly more conscious than her brother, she was still pretty much out of it. Shivering and stone-cold to the touch, her stress factor was very high. I decided at once to take Boycat to the cage first and then come back for her. Carefully, I pulled the canvas sheet out from under her and ran back to Boycat.

'Jimmy,' I said, panting slightly, 'I want to get Boycat into the cage first and then come back for Poep. Can you monitor her for me?' Poepface was far riskier to handle and since I was the only person she trusted and she was familiar with the way I touched and held her, I wanted to be the one to carry her. Acknowledging Jimmy's nod, I felt a bit better and, after giving me a hand in lifting Boycat on to the canvas sheet, he walked back to the chopper.

'Sam,' I urged, pointing to the sheet, 'come and give me a hand.' Our new camp assistant had probably never seen a live leopard before, let alone one at such close quarters, but he dutifully stepped forward. 'If you grab those two corners I'll take these.'

Together, we carried my beautiful boy down the small game trail to the cage where we slowly lowered the canvas to the ground while Anthony Bannister continued taking photos. Then, leaving Sam outside the cage, I bent down to pick Boycat up, hoping that in his confused state he wouldn't nail me with his unsheathed claws. The last time I had tried to lift him just a month earlier he had spun around in my arms and almost taken my head off, missing my face by millimetres. Kneeling down next to him I slipped my arm beneath his belly and chest to raise him off the ground and lift him into the cage.

'Okay, let's go,' I said to Sam after making sure Boycat was as comfortable as possible for now. Closing the door behind me, I turned to Anthony and telling him not under any circumstances to enter the cage until I had returned with Poep, I quickly ran back up the path.

Back at the helicopter, I climbed through the back door and took hold of Poepface, sliding my arm beneath her belly and chest and heaving her off the floor. As I was carrying her sedated body to the cage she lashed out with her claws, shearing into my skin as she attempted to gain some sort of grip. Anthony held the door open for me to enter the cage and then followed me in to take more photos while I gently laid my little girl beside her brother on the canvas sheet and softly kissed her on the top of her head. She couldn't focus properly and hissed when she felt the movement of her brother's body against her, not recognising him, and urinated involuntarily. I quickly grabbed the blankets I had put inside the cage earlier that morning and covered her shivering body while she attempted to raise her head which was flopping from side to side.

Boycat was struggling to sit up, wobbling to and fro as he half managed to get up and look around the cage with hugely fearful eyes. I spread a second thick blanket over him. Poep too looked around her, wearing the same fearful and confused look as the day she had arrived at Londolozi almost a year earlier. Feeling my heart growing cold, I turned to Anthony Bannister and asked him to leave. I didn't want anything to add to the cubs' stress and I wanted them to realise they had each other as they slowly came round.

I vaguely heard the sound of the chopper growing distant as I stroked Boycat and Poep, reassuring them that the hardest part was now over. It pained me to see my two babies rendered so powerless and I wanted to try to get them to understand that I was there and that they had nothing to fear. After a while, when I thought they were a little calmer, I got up and left the cage to allow them to rest and sleep off the effects of the sedation.

When I returned three quarters of an hour later, Boycat had recovered considerably. Walking around to the front of the cage, I saw him peering through a gap in the thorny foliage that covered the metal bars and watching me coming towards the door. Both cubs were still somewhat unsteady on their legs and moved around the cage as if in a drunken stupor, but I was hugely relieved to see that Poep's eyes had reverted back to normal. She chuffed at me in greeting as I went inside and after inspecting the water bowls I noticed with some satisfaction that they had already had a little drink. Sitting down beside them, I gave Boycat a good rub and as he curled his tail around my leg a massive load fell off me. My babies were safe and had arrived at their new home.

I checked on the cubs again a few times before nightfall, slightly uneasy about them being so far away from my tent during the dangerous dark hours of night. Had I fixed all the gaps properly? Were Boycat and Poep secure inside? I wondered what they made of the incessant sounds of hippos in the river and lay awake with the image in my mind of Poep's scared, terrifyingly haunted eyes. I never wanted to see them like that ever again.

AT FIRST LIGHT I jumped out of bed and, pushing my legs into a pair of shorts and my feet into shoes, I zipped open the tent flap and walked hurriedly towards the cage. Late the night before I had heard a pride of lions squabbling over a kill about a kilometre or two north-west of camp and, listening to the loud, throaty snarls and rumbles I was immediately awake and on full alert. Trotting eagerly down the trail, I reached the cage a few minutes later to find that, uncharacteristically, Karin was already there and had just opened the door for the cubs to come out.

'STOP!' I yelled, sprinting the last ten metres. 'What the hell are you doing? You can't just dump them out there! You'll get them killed right away!'

I was furious and snapped at her mercilessly. I knew she meant well but sometimes she didn't fully understand how dangerous it was for the cubs to be allowed free in this wild environment. The one hundred metre distance between the cubs and my tent had been deliberate on my part because I wanted to initiate the release process as gradually as possible, allowing Boycat and Poep to familiarise themselves with the immediate area around camp before venturing any further on the island. I had discussed my ideas with Nick in considerable depth before he left Londolozi, telling him that I wanted to keep them inside the cage for a few days before letting them explore. Nick had agreed that a soft release was the best and safest way to introduce the cubs to the Luangwa Valley where there would be many new smells and sounds for them to get used to. I also felt very strongly that the cubs had to understand that we lived here and that this new camp was a place of safety to which they could return if either of them found themselves in trouble and needed a refuge.

I first allowed the cubs out early on the morning of 12 April 1994, three full days after they had arrived. I opened the door wide and stepped back to allow them the opportunity to come outside and start investigating the immediate vicinity of their new home. Now that they had had a few days to settle in I was less worried about them exploring this unfamiliar territory, having learnt a long time ago that if they sensed anything dangerous close by they would be wary and prefer to stay inside. The choice in the end was always theirs. After just a few seconds, two little leopard faces peered curiously around the door, glancing about them slightly nervously. After a few seconds of hesitation Boycat came forward and instinctively dashed into the highest reaches of a tall Natal mahogany tree to the left of the cage and scanned the surroundings from his lofted position. Poepface, usually always the one to head straight for the trees, completely ignored the small stand of mahoganies. Giving me a playful bat on the legs as she emerged from the cage, she began to pad slowly across the grassy clearing. *Slowly*, I thought. Everything must happen slowly, slowly from now on. It was good to see them showing a natural apprehension for their completely unfamiliar environment and I knew they possessed a strong sense of self-preservation.

Still, I wished I could sit them down and explain exactly what they had to look out for.

For the next few days I kept Boycat and Poep close to camp and entertained them with endless games of soccer and flicking a rope with an old shoe dangling from its end, deciding to take them on their first proper outing on Saturday. Following a few metres behind the cubs Karin and I traipsed after Boycat when he headed purposefully to the north bank of the island where he began investigating the tree line. Meticulously sniffing every bush and clump of grass, the cubs suddenly noticed a herd of impala and puku feeding on some tall grass across the Luangwa River on one of the sandbanks that had recently been exposed. Crouching low, Boycat slowly began to stalk them, until suddenly he sprang from his patch of riverbank and hurtled in their direction. The herd snorted in alarm and then froze and stared at him from across the water. Feeling exposed and a little intimidated, Boycat instantly crept into a thicket to watch the two herds from the cover of the bush until gradually they drifted further afield and disappeared from sight.

Losing interest, the cubs began exploring an area of long grass to the east of the river bank where Boycat, hearing a rustle in the vegetation, dived into a thicket and almost flushed a baby puku. Poep, who had been momentarily distracted as she sniffed at some bushes, looked up and grew immediately anxious when she could not see her brother. Standing rigidly, she scrutinised the area nervously and seemed visibly relieved when he reappeared. Sticking close to Boycat, she made sure not to allow him out of sight a second time. All in all, I was very satisfied with the way the cubs had responded and after a good few hours of exploring I suggested to Karin that we return to camp, luring the cubs back with fresh meat. Locking them back inside the cage to give them a chance to have a lunchtime snooze, I got ready to fetch JV from the GMA side to do a film shoot with Boycat later that afternoon.

Trudging across the wide expanse of sand to the south of camp I pushed the dinghy into the water and, seizing the shovel to row across the river, I leaned perilously low over the front to ensure I didn't accidentally puncture the rubber sides, while trying hard not to think about the number of crocodiles that could well be watching me from the deeper water. One powerful explosive leap and any respectable South Luangwa croc could have half my body down its throat in a matter of seconds. Paddling on alternate sides, I navigated a distance upstream to compensate for the river's strong westward flow so that I would land more or less where I wanted to on the opposite bank. About five minutes later I reached the opposite shore and, after shaking hands with JV who had been waiting for me, we made the same perilous journey back across the river together.

It was already late in the afternoon when JV finished filming and I dropped him back off at the GMA and, leaving him to drive back to Xingi's camp further downstream, I rowed back again. Having reached the floodplain for the second time that day, I dragged the dinghy up on to the sandbank and started making my way back to camp on foot, sweating profusely. Despite the late hour, it was still boiling hot and when I reached the pan about fifty metres before the island's southern bank I relished the idea of cooling off a bit. Shoeless, I waded into the water; first my ankles, then my calves and then my thighs until I was about waist-high into the pool. I was thinking about the cubs and wondering for how long I'd be able to persuade them to follow us back to the camp at night, dreading the first evening they remained out alone, and was somewhat absent-mindedly putting one foot after the other. About halfway across the water I stepped on something that felt like a patch of burnt grass. Suddenly alert, but not immediately fearful, it took me a second or two to realise that any burnt vegetation would feel soft beneath the water, and that there was a distinct possibility that my foot was resting on the back of a crocodile.

For a heart-stopping moment I did nothing. Since I hadn't yet put the full weight of my body down on to whatever I was standing on, I balanced somewhat precariously on my left leg while my mind started processing my predicament. Okay, I thought. I am probably standing on a crocodile; now what do I do? Remaining as composed as I could under the circumstances, I calmly tried to make sense of the situation. First, there were a few questions to be answered. On what part of the crocodile's body was my foot resting, and what would the croc do if I took my foot off its back? Ever so carefully feeling around with my toes, I tried to ascertain whether there were large or small scales in the vicinity of my foot, knowing that the bigger and upright plate-like armour appeared closer to the tail. If my toe detected smaller scales I was probably standing very near the croc's head, which was a rather disconcerting thought.

Identifying a prominent plate and feeling slightly relieved to have this small advantage, I remained dead still for the longest half-minute of my life thinking all the while how ridiculous it was to mull over the details of a crocodile's anatomy while actually standing upon one. But since I couldn't exactly stay there all day, I had to initiate some kind of action. Not knowing what else to do, I pressed my foot down on to the crocodile's back the tiniest bit and feeling the slightest of movements beneath it, I leapt forward just seconds before something discharged itself from the water to my left. Thrusting its tail as a rudder, the ancient reptile rocketed away to the far side of the pool and, catching a glimpse of its serrated back, I estimated it to be a small seven footer. Still, I was impressed by the sheer force with which the young crocodile splashed through the shallow water and counted myself lucky not to have been slapped by the tail. Laughing nervously when I was back on dry ground, I continued my walk back to the island.

Too tired to write in my notebook that night, I opened the page after the last entry four days earlier and with a slightly cynical smile entered the sentence, *Stood on crocodile after taking JV back this afternoon.* A few days passed before I returned to continue my record of the cubs' progress.

> Saw brown snake eagle with snake, Lillian's lovebirds, crowned cranes, a big flock of 20+ spur-winged geese two days ago. Saw another croc to north of the island where the river splits. Boycat has begun scent marking

the area and Poep is much more relaxed. Both came back to camp after a long walk without too much hassle but knew they wanted to stay out longer. Will keep bringing them back as long as they are happy to come. Played darts with Cha, beating her only narrowly today. Saw two hippos fighting in the river at last light as Cha and I bathed in one of the shallower pools. This place is so beautiful makes your jaw drop. Feels like you could discover dinosaurs here.

More long walks with the cubs over the next days. Saw two big crocs running through the water on the north bank. Was tired last night after heavy wind blew against the canvas, knocking over the paraffin lamp, lucky, as could have had a fire. Went to sleep to the sound of howling storm. Heard a bit of rain during the night and lions calling to the east of camp. Was up latish to let cubs out. Boycat led the walk, heading west, where they hadn't explored before. Cubs played on the sandbank then went north into the long grass zone to check out the banks of the river. I couldn't get them to follow me back to camp; hope they're ready for this. Elmon dropped off two impalas yesterday, so I went back to drag a chunk of the carcass to where the cubs were. Boy was immediately interested so dragged it all the way back again with him running behind. Poep stayed out. Only managed to lure her back to camp later that afternoon. Boy gave me a good gash on the shoulder later while we were playing; he's almost my shoulder height when up on his hind legs. Poep scratched my hand, but only trying to get food. Don't think I will be able to get my babies to come back to the cage for long any more. Am worried for them. Will kill me if anything happens to either of them. They've become such beautiful leopards. Won't be long now before they'll want to stay out all night; scares me.

IT WAS QUITE surprising to see how quickly Boycat and Poep adapted to their new home and how drawn they were to the north bank where the river still divided our island from the mainland of the national park. Karin and I often lost sight of the cubs in the long grass only to find them relaxing innocently on one of the sandbanks after we'd conducted an agonising search. Increasingly, I noticed Boycat sitting on the river bank and staring at the water for long periods of time. But eventually he would stand up and move inland.

Three days later, after another restless night worrying about the cubs, I followed Boycat and Poep back to the north bank. Something compelled them to return day after day to the point where, as the days wore on, Boycat grew ever more reluctant to come back to camp. The night before Karin and I had managed to bring them back a short time before nightfall and whereas Poep had happily gone inside the cage by herself, Boycat hadn't wanted to; I'd literally had to give him a shove and close the door behind him.

The dry winter season began gradually to set in and the floodwaters around the island started slowly to recede, exposing new floodplains and island sandbanks which opened up new shallow pans enticing Boycat into the water. It was on a Saturday morning, almost exactly two weeks after the cubs arrived in Zambia, that Karin and I were once again following Boycat and Poep towards the north bank. As we came out of the long grass at the river bank a rush of cool air played lightly with the water below the banks and watching the cubs pacing up and down the river bank almost compulsively, I nudged Karin on the shoulder. Something was different today.

Peering restlessly at the surface of the water, Boycat and Poep's gaze intensified and, barely able to speak as I comprehended what was going on, my heart began to pound. They were going to cross. Patrolling up and down the bank, Boycat and Poep stopped intermittently and stared at the water before continuing to pace once more. For about ten minutes the cubs hesitated as if their minds were warning them against what their instinct was urging them to do. Boycat was fidgeting nervously despite his natural passion for water. Most days during our daily walks I'd watch him wallowing in shallow pools that were increasingly drying up, but it was obvious that he was aware that the river was quite different to a mere pan and that it spelt potential danger. Poep too appeared anxious. Never one to enjoy getting wet, it was as if she knew what her brother was up to and would have to choose between two evils if he decided to cross. Casting her gaze from the river back to her brother she flicked her tail in the air, unsure of the situation. And then, as if triggered by a silent signal, Boycat took the lead and started to move in the direction of the water.

With our hearts in our mouths, Karin and I watched as Boycat scrambled down the dry crumbly bank and slipped silently into the water, wading in until his long sleek body was submerged to the shoulders. Then he began to swim. Squeaking nervously, Poep watched her brother moving through the water, the distance between them increasing every moment. We stood frozen to the ground, watching him negotiate the crocodile-infested river. Karin, panicking, pulled a 9mm pistol from the pocket of her shorts, loaded it and aimed it at Boycat in case something came up out of the water and grabbed him.

'Put that down,' I growled nervously. 'You're not going to change a thing if a croc gets him now and if you fire that thing you'll risk shooting him!' She looked at me and then put the weapon away, staring wordlessly as Boycat moved through the twelve to fifteen metres of water. Those were surely the longest moments of our lives. When he reached the southern bank of the mainland safely and rose from the river with sheets of water streaming down his body we both heaved a huge sigh of relief.

Ouugwh ouugwh. Stepping cautiously across a strip of small pebbles and stones that had been pushed on to higher ground during previous flood seasons, Boycat turned and called for his sister. Still apprehensive, Poepface replied with a low, throaty rumble. She stared hard at the water before negotiating her way down to the bank to enter the river. With my heart in my mouth, and powerless to change anything that might happen now, I said a silent prayer. Adrenalin raced through my veins as I watched my little girl swim across the water until she too emerged safe and sound on the shores of the mainland.

'That's it!' I said, turning to Karin. 'I'm going after them!'

Crashing down the bank I plunged into the cool flowing water holding my loaded light automatic R1 rifle above my head and pointed downwards in anticipation of letting off a shot the moment I felt the slightest movement around my feet. With the water rising against my legs I felt the soggy mud-like layers of sand levelling out when the water was halfway to my chest and, hearing splashing behind me, I realised that Karin had decided to follow.

Finally, the soft sand beneath my feet began to rise as we neared the opposite bank and I emerged with Karin close behind. Sopping wet, we stood on the shores of the South Luangwa National Park and looked around us, and despite my anxiety about the cubs I couldn't help noticing that it was overwhelmingly beautiful. Few, if any, people came here and you could sense a wilderness that parks and reserves managed by the hands of man never quite achieved. Scanning the undergrowth beyond the flood line, I peered into the bush for any sign of Boycat and Poep, but it was as if they had vanished into thin air. We began searching immediately, but found that it was virtually impossible to track them across the wide band of rocks and stones. A dry riverbed wound deep into the bush, penetrating the dense foliage like an artery and, finding evidence of their tracks there, leading away from the river in a north-easterly direction, we followed the spoor for a few hundred metres inland through riverine shrub. It was here that the ground became hard and their paw prints disappeared. I felt myself stiffen as I stared into the thick bush; we could go no further. Feeling my heart grow cold with hopelessness and defeat, I remained quiet for a few moments before turning to Karin. She shrugged her shoulders.

Together we made our way back to camp in silence. Battling with emotions of turmoil, admiration, worry and triumph, I felt confused and shocked. Surely this couldn't be it? Surely they were just exploring and would come back? I couldn't think of anything but the cubs and, incapable of just sitting around camp, I got to my feet a few hours later. 'I'm going,' I told Cha. 'I can't just sit here and wonder.' She nodded, offering to come too, so we called Karin and prepared to leave right away.

Asking Sam to keep an eye on things, the three of us hurried back to the spot on the north bank where the cubs had crossed the river. I scanned the ground for tracks in case the cubs had returned to the island but when I failed to find any fresh spoor, I made a quick decision. 'They're still on the mainland,' I said, sitting down on the ground and taking my shoes off. 'I'm going back there.'

'I'll come too,' Cha said bravely, but I was having none of it. 'Forget it!' I said. 'This river is potentially fatal and there is no way I'll let you risk your life.' She agreed somewhat reluctantly to stay behind and sat down on the bank while Karin and I waded in a second time.

After crossing the flood line of pebbles on the other side I randomly picked a narrow game trail and headed into the thick vegetation, every inch of which we combed for the next two and a half hours without finding a single paw print. Exhausted and drained by anxiety, I peered up at the sky through a gap in the forest canopy. It was getting late. Soon the sun would begin to drop towards the horizon and it would start getting dark. I didn't want the day to end; I didn't want to spend a night in camp without knowing that Boycat and Poepface were safe. But I also had to remain cool-headed and could not afford to act irresponsibly. Lions, leopards, hyenas – they would all soon rouse themselves to roam the night under the treacherous mantle of darkness.

'We'd better get back,' I told Karin. 'I don't think we're going to find them.'

My head was spinning and I felt a dull weakness descend over me as we traipsed back to the river and arrived on a sandy bank a little to the east of where we had entered the bush. The first thing I saw as we came out into the open was Cha who immediately stood up and began frantically waving her arms over her head to attract our attention. 'Graham!' she called cupping her hands over her mouth. 'She's there! Poep! Look behind you. *There! There!*'

Turning on our heels, Karin and I peered into the greenery to see Poepface walking out of the thick foliage in our direction. My heart soared. *'Poepity!'* Hurrying towards her I fell beside her on the sand, feeling her sleek fur rubbing along my legs and running the back of my hand over her head and back. 'Where have you been, my little baby? And where is your brother?'

I wanted her to come back with me across the river to spend the night safely in the cage, but after following me the few metres to the edge of the river she stopped and withdrew sharply.

'Come, girl, come,' I coaxed, but she was nervous and refused to cross.

I was torn between wanting to stay with her and obeying my common sense to go back to the camp. There is no way she'll come, I thought. She won't come back with me without her brother. And she so feared the water. The only reason she'd made the crossing at all was because she hated being separated from Boycat, who she loved more than anything in the world.

Watching the river and the fading light, and then turning to Karin, I read her questioning gaze. I once again looked at Poep, knowing that there was nothing more distressing to me than leaving her behind, alone by herself in the wilderness. Yet I couldn't risk Poep crossing back with me only to change her mind while we were walking back to camp. What if she then decided to brave the river alone to look for her brother? Was I just being selfish?

Giving Karin a brief nod, I swallowed hard and turning back to the Luangwa River we once again entered the water. I couldn't think. I just waded in, my emotions suspended in a cobweb of despair and, after climbing up the opposite bank and giving Cha a hug, I still lingered while she and Karin prepared to head back to camp. Across the darkening water I saw a leopard, a beautiful young female, stalking sandpipers in the shallows. Crouching low, her white furry belly resting on the soft sand, eyes bright and alert and ears pricked, she flicked her tail as she tried to single out an individual straggler, oblivious of me, the human on the other side of the river who loved her more than life itself. Finally I turned my back. This was the beginning of a new life for her and for her brother. And for me.

My babies had turned into wild leopards.

16
BOYCAT

Standing on the north bank of the island shortly after daybreak, I scrutinised the water for any ripples before convincing myself it was safe to wade in. As if frozen in time, a massive crocodile was sunning itself at the edge of the river a short distance downstream but I reckoned he was far enough away for me to reach the opposite bank unscathed. I *have* to change my crossing point, I thought as I wallowed chest-high into the water. This was just too dangerous. I knew that crocodiles watched for repetitive behaviour, lying submerged and waiting for an unsuspecting victim to enter the water. I hoped the cubs knew this too.

On the other side of the river I began hunting for tracks, staying out for several hours and searching everywhere I could possibly go. But Boycat and Poep were nowhere to be found, not so much as a single pug mark or flash of gold and black rosetted fur.

By mid-morning the temperature had shot up and it became too hot to stay out. I went back to the river to look for a suitable place to cross back to the island, hoping I hadn't accidentally chosen a particularly deep section. Relieved that I was still in one piece, I scrambled up on to the island and trudged back to camp, shaking my head when Cha approached me with enquiring eyes.

Where *were* they? Dejectedly, I picked through a late breakfast of cold tuna and tinned mixed vegetables in the shade of the tall mahogany that towered over the tent. I wasn't particularly hungry, but Cha insisted I have something to eat, so half-heartedly I finished what was on my plate before going to rinse it in the kitchen. Then, in an effort to escape from my worries, I went to the tent to find the fascinating book I had begun reading about the history of wind by Lyall Watson. But after only half a page I put it down again, finding it impossible to distract my mind. My ears were alert for the smallest of sounds that might betray the whereabouts of the cubs – tree squirrels' bird-like alarm chatter or the screeches of a troop of monkeys. I had only to hear the tiniest sound to be up on my feet investigating.

But the bush was quiet. Unable to sit still, I decided to join Sam who needed to get a few supplies from his village in the GMA, a two and a half hour walk through the bush with heat, dust and tsetse flies for company. Still, it was better than just hanging around the camp and, taking a six-pack of beers to swap for two chickens in case the cubs decided to come back hungry, we left. By the time we got back it was almost nightfall. I went to the kitchen to radio JV at Xingi's camp to let him know I hadn't been able to find the cubs before going back outside to join the others at the fire. Cha had made a simple supper of potato mash with tinned sausages and chopped tomato and onion mix, but as I sat down I barely heard what she and Karin were discussing. John threw another log on the crackling flames and joined in the conversation but my mind was solely on the cubs. The sky grew increasingly dark with just a mist of fine stars and I felt stifled in my own body; a prisoner of anxiety. It was their second night out and I didn't even know if they had survived the first.

I woke early the next morning to a series of bellowing roars thundering across the valley. Uncertain whether the lions were calling from the island or across the river I jumped out of bed, dressed hastily and grabbed my loaded 30.06 rifle. It was just light enough to see and as I hastened back to the northern bank, I narrowed my eyes and peered over the water before picking a spot a few hundred metres west of my last crossing point. The Luangwa River sparkled like a diamond necklace in the pink light of dawn and the valley was filled with the promise of another beautiful day. To the east, a bulky shape moved across a wide sandbank and I recognised the dark silhouette of a lone bull hippo plodding back to the river after a night's foraging.

Back on the mainland of the national park, I continued the previous day's search further east where I found a leopard's footprints in a muddy patch beside a small tributary heading inland. They were Boycat's. Bending down, I examined the prints which appeared to be a day old. There was no sign of Poep, but as I very much doubted that she had left her brother to cross the river back to the island, I figured that both cubs were still on the mainland. I followed Boy's tracks until they hit dry ground and I lost them and, standing still, I tried to put myself in their position. Where would *I* have gone if I were them?

Closing my eyes, I tuned into the bush, listening for anything that might hint at the movements of two leopards padding through the forest. I could hear branches breaking to the north and there was the faraway sound of elephants trumpeting. Closer by, a pair of Egyptian geese flew overhead, squawking noisily, and I could hear the faint purling of the Luangwa River as its waters flowed gently downstream. There was nothing to suggest that Boycat and Poep were anywhere nearby.

By day three I was desperate. I knew that I would have to let them go, but couldn't give up looking for them until I knew that they were safe. Once again, I went to the north bank and made the perilous crossing, but again I had no success. I'd barely returned to camp when out of nowhere a troop of baboons began grunting, barking and screaming on the mainland north-west of camp. My heart lifted and I ran all the way back, certain that at last I was finally going to find them. But by the time I had crossed the river the baboons had gone and the bush was once again silent.

'*Booooooooy!! Pooooeeeep!!*' I called their names over and over again for more than two hours while I traipsed the forest floor and searched in vain. Eventually I had to give up. There was nothing I could do but wait.

A few hours later I was walking back to camp from the long-drop when I saw something lying in the shade of my tent wall. I could scarcely believe my eyes – it was Boycat! I rushed up to him, giving two short puffs in greeting, but as he raised his face towards me I noticed immediately that he appeared quite tense. Chuffing back at me, he got up as I sank to my knees beside him to rub the fur beneath his jaw.

'Hello, my big, beautiful Boy!' I cooed. 'Where have you been? Where is your sister?' Looking into his stunning green eyes I instantly saw a change, a loss of innocence that spoke of new, uncertain experiences in an unfamiliar world. With a sense of shock I realised that Boycat's eyes mirrored those of a wild leopard and that the carefree young prankster I knew was no longer a cub. Boycat had grown into a beautiful adult leopard.

Finding him something to eat, I left him to settle under a bush with his meal to feed in peace and, hearing someone yelling for attention from the GMA, I hurried down to the river bank. JV was waving his arms and calling for help from across the river and so I rowed across in the dinghy to help him push his vehicle out of a patch of thick mud and was also able to give him the news that Boycat had just shown up at camp.

'Ah, man!' He beamed with relief. 'That is such great news, Graham!' Taking off his bush hat, he wiped the perspiration from his brow. 'I'm on my way to get an impala for Xingi. If you'll give me an hour or so and then meet me back here, I'll bring you some meat for Boycat too.' True to his word, he reappeared on the other side of the river later that afternoon and, after thanking him, I dragged half an impala into the dinghy and rowed back to the island. Carrying the carcass over my shoulders, I walked across the floodplain and back to camp only to find that Boycat had gone.

Disappointed, I cut the meat up, stored a few large chunks in the gas fridge and walked to a sandbank some distance from camp to leave the head for the vultures. I'd hardly gone far when I saw four white-headed vultures, six hooded vultures and one lappet-faced vulture already riding the thermals high above me, circling overhead and ready to descend on the spoils.

Since Boycat and Poepface were only a year old and still largely inexperienced at catching prey I wanted to make sure they didn't go hungry while they were learning to survive by themselves during these early days of independence. So I took a large chunk of the impala from the fridge and carried it to a twenty-foot Natal mahogany tree not far from their cage, planning to hoist it into a fork in the trunk. I'd just got there when a small sound distracted me and, turning around, I saw a big leopard bounding out of the bush towards me. On full alert, I drew a sharp breath before recognising Boycat, who had obviously seen me approaching with the meat and, always keen for a game, now launched a playful attack. It was incredible to me that, even though he was almost an adult, we still shared such a close bond of trust and affection.

I gave him a piece of meat and then, slinging the rest of the meat over my shoulder, started to climb the tree, but I had only gone a few feet when I felt a heavy tug which caused me to lose my balance and fall to the ground. Turning to face a mischievous Boycat, I began to laugh.

'Hey!' I admonished him. 'You can't just claw the meat off my shoulder!' I stopped for a while and stroked his flanks before making my way up into the tree again, only for Boycat to rear up on his hindquarters and once again hook his claws into the meat. He pulled me out of the tree like this four or five times before I gave up my plan. 'All right, my Boy,' I relented. 'I know all about your games. Have it your way!' Giving him the rest of the meat, I stayed with him while he finished his meal and then moved lethargically into the bushes for a rest.

When I returned to check on him later in the afternoon he had gone. 'Come, let's go for a walk,' I said, taking Cha's hand. 'Maybe we'll find him heading back to Poepface.'

We returned to the north bank but I couldn't find any of Boycat's tracks so we walked eastwards where a few recently exposed sandbanks had formed a land bridge to the mainland of the park. Crossing these, Cha and I found ourselves on the river bank where to our left a wide sandy gully bled deeply into the bush. Turning right, we entered a patch of ten-foot high grass and walked along a narrow hippo trail that opened up into a very pretty little clearing and, deciding that this would be a perfect picnic place, we settled down to enjoy the few beers and peanuts I had brought with me.

'Booooooycat! Poeeeeep!' I called every now and again, imagining how perfect everything would be if they joined us.

But the cubs didn't show and, as if reading my thoughts when the sun started slowly dropping towards the horizon, Cha touched my shoulder lightly and said softly, 'I'm sure Poepface is fine, Graham. Boycat also came back …' I nodded and got up, offering her my hand. 'Okay, let's go back.'

As I was pulling Cha to her feet I heard a loud swishing in the grass and turning towards the sound I caught a glimpse of a tawny, black-tipped tail racing over the sea of vegetation towards us. I immediately jerked Cha behind me, grabbed, loaded and aimed the rifle faster than I would have believed possible and, peering over the barrel with one eye closed, I saw the lioness break from cover. For a split second she glared at me with fiery yellow eyes before realising that she had lost the advantage of surprise and her intentions had been foiled. Veering to one side in a single swift movement, she turned tail and bolted back into the long grass.

I kept the rifle at eye-level, alert to the possibility of a second charge and not wanting to fire a warning shot into the air because if that failed to intimidate her there was a good chance that she might attack before I had the chance to reload and fire again. We waited nervously for several minutes without hearing another sound, which presented me with another predicament. Since the lioness had disappeared in the same direction we'd have to follow back to camp, I had no way of knowing whether she was lying low nearby in anticipation of another ambush. Looking up at the sky I also realised that, with sunset less than hour away, we couldn't afford to wait much longer.

'Let's give her another few minutes,' I said, lowering the rifle. 'Give her a chance to move away.' Noticing a tall termite mound nearby, I walked towards it and scrambled up on to it and, peering over the vegetation from the elevated vantage point, I saw a tawny shape slipping away through the sea of grass. 'Come, let's go,' I said, grabbing Cha by the hand. 'We'd better get out of here quickly.'

I FOUND BOYCAT again early the following morning a short distance from where I'd left him the day before. Together we watched the sun's golden rays wash over the Luangwa Valley as I sat close beside him for a number of hours until the heat became too much to bear. Returning in the early afternoon with Cha, we found him lying in more or less the same spot, sleeping in the shade of a dense thicket.

'Here you go, my Boy,' I whispered softly as I gave him the best part of the impala leg. This time he allowed me to hoist the remainder of the meat into a tree and, leaving him looking comfortable as he settled himself for the night, we returned to camp.

By sunrise the following morning, he was gone. Following his footprints in a northerly direction I arrived at a small sandbank carpeted with tall grass where it became increasingly difficult to follow his tracks. Swishing through the grass, I swept my eyes left and right until, about ten metres ahead of me, I saw a leopard's face pop up over the grass. Boycat! Delighted, I went to greet him and as I approached a second leopard raised her head to peer up over the vegetation. Instantly, my heart soared – it was Poepface! Giving a triumphant yell, I read the briefest hint of uncertainty in her eyes which disappeared after two quick chuffs when recognition flowed back into her mind and her gaze softened.

Shaking her head, she jumped up and both cubs bounded over to me, leaping around excitedly and playfully batting my leg. In the excitement Boycat began tackling his smaller sister and our reunion turned into one big game. I started laughing, at last feeling the tension of the last four days ebb from my body like water on to desert sand. She was here; she was safe! The three of us played together for a long time, with me pretending not to see them as they stalked me through the high grass, giving them the chance to ambush me. I hoped that the cubs would follow me so I could give Poep a good solid meal and, slowly leading them in the direction of camp, I started walking back, happier than I'd been in what seemed ages, with two gleeful leopards bounding after me. Back at camp, Boycat and Poepface happily devoured the last of the meat rations and I sat with them, savouring every moment of my time with them. Later that evening after the cubs had left camp, I went to sleep with a smile on my face, relieved that my little girl was all right and that some of my worries had finally been assuaged.

I found the cubs together every day for the next week, within a ten-metre radius of a different stand of Natal mahoganies further inland in which I had been stringing fresh impala meat for them. I had had to change the position of the meat because I found the tracks of a huge crocodile beside the tree where Boycat had jumped on me. I couldn't believe my eyes; it would have made sense if I'd found hyena or lion spoor, or even another leopard, but to imagine that a large croc had been attracted by the smell of whatever Boycat might have left was quite incredible.

It took me all the following day to find Boycat and Poep, but I finally came across both of them moving east in the direction of camp during the late afternoon. Walking with them, the three of us arrived in the early afternoon, with both cubs in high spirits. Playfully, Boycat flew straight to our tent where Cha was resting and hurled himself on to the bed, giving her a bit of a start for which I had to tell him off. Undeterred, he then joined his sister and they proceeded to thrash our laundry, hooking their claws into our shirts, shorts, socks and towels and ripping them off the washing line to drag them all the way through camp. It was good to see that some things hadn't changed.

A WALL OF black, brooding clouds was rolling in over the valley, painting the river in a strangely beautiful surreal light. In the distance, strong bursts of wind were gusting and, as the pockets of air began howling towards us, I knew we were in for a big storm.

Everyone in camp quickly secured any loose items, checked the tie-down lines and huddled inside their tents with flaps tightly closed and, glancing at the book I had been reading, *Heaven's Breath*, it seemed ridiculously appropriate. Shortly after dark the storm hit the island. Whirling and wailing around the tent walls, the gusts were so powerful that I was convinced that Cha and I were about to lift off inside the tent. The rumblings of rolling thunder and crashing lightning filled the darkness outside while we shivered inside and I was more than a little surprised that the cupboard remained standing. An hour or so later, once the wind had passed, the rain began to fall, beating down hard against the canvas. Finally, as the storm passed and the pelting rain mellowed into no more than a quiet pitter-patter, we relaxed a little. Worried about how the cubs might be faring in this weather, I prayed that they had found a safe place.

By morning the sky had cleared into a glowing pink, soft and gentle as if to

By morning the sky had cleared into a glowing pink, soft and gentle as if to neutralise the previous night's violence. I jumped out of bed and, persuading Cha to come with me, we walked towards the south bank where we saw three lions lazily eyeing a hippo wanting to get out of the water nearby. We didn't find the cubs there, but spotted them later after following their tracks to an area of thick shrubs not far from camp.

A few days later, just before dawn, Boycat and Poep showed up in camp by themselves, padding quietly along the tents and giving the young Zambian man who'd taken over Sam's duties while he was away the fright of his life. I was still in bed when I heard him screaming blue murder and, hurrying outside, found him trembling a few metres away from the kitchen tent while the two leopards stalked him mercilessly in a classic pincer movement. I suppressed a snort of laughter and quickly ran forward to help the poor guy.

Boycat looked smug and mischievous, happy to have attracted attention and I good-naturedly told him off while trying to distract him and his sister away from the kitchen. Scrutinising their condition, I thought that they had lost a bit of weight.

Satisfied and in the mood for some fun after I had gone back to the kitchen to fetch them some meat, Boycat's eyes followed Cha as she passed him on the way to the long-drop. After taking cover behind some small bushes, he began to stalk her from behind but luckily I saw what he was up to and, grabbing a clod of earth, I followed him until the moment he was about to pounce, when I threw it just behind his bum to startle him. He jumped and gave me a dirty look for spoiling his plans. I didn't think he would ever intentionally hurt Cha or anyone else, but he was just too big for this sort of thing now.

'Here,' I said when she came back. 'Take this cup of water and next time he is naughty you throw it in his face. That should put a stop to his games.'

me walking towards the toilet and, seizing his chance, he bolted over to our tent to scare Cha. He entered sneakily, trying to remain invisible before jumping on Cha, but he was unprepared for the cup of water that she chucked right in his face and leapt back again. Not certain how to react he stopped short and, embarrassed, bounded outside where he soon regained his cool cat image. Knowing that he would most certainly give it another try, I warned Cha to watch out because he would try and get back at her for having one up on him, the way he always did. Sure enough, a short time later, Boycat went around the back of our tent and saw Cha lying on the bed reading. He crouched down and then leapt, his front feet against the fly screen, and standing up on his back legs he hooked his claws into the gauze. He got another cup of water for that and for a third attempt to give her a fright until he finally got sick of getting his face wet and he slouched off grumpily.

A few days later, just before the sun set over the valley and we withdrew into our tents for the night, the cubs made their way back to the island after chasing a herd of puku on the sandbank east of camp. By the time it was dark, tragedy had struck. The following morning, as the pink light dawned over the horizon and a new day began, my Poepface was alone and the world had lost a beautiful, brave young leopard.

Boycat was dead.

17
POEPFACE

She was sitting in front of a small line of trees staring at the water on the western bank of the river and she looked tense and frightened. And that's when I knew. She should have been hiding when she heard me coming, concealing herself in the vegetation in anticipation of pouncing on me and playfully batting my legs. Something was terribly wrong. The Poepface I saw sitting by the water was a shadow of the leopard I knew.

Slowing down as I approached her, I asked if she were all right but, unusually, she did not react to the sound of my voice. Only when I had come to within a few feet did she respond. She spun around and, her eyes cold with accusation, she took a swipe at my face with her claws out. That said it all. A violent pain shot through me and I knew my little man had gone. *No.* My heart cried silently, *No.No.No.No ... Not Boycat! Oh God, please, not my little man!*

My ears were ringing and my stomach churned as my mind desperately attempted to make sense of the senseless. Her turmoil, fear and confusion – her preoccupation with the river ... It must have been a submerged crocodile that had seized her brother and pulled him down into the depths while he and Poep were crossing back to the island the night before.

'I'm sorry,' I whispered, sitting down beside her and feeling the tears spill down my cheeks. 'I am so, so sorry I wasn't here to protect him.'

There was no reaction. She just refused to take her eyes off the water and I felt gutted, guilty, realising with horror that she must have seen it happen right beside her. *She saw her brother being taken.* My heart felt heavy and I felt myself grow cold. Only three days earlier a man from the local village had been seized by a crocodile while he was standing up to his shoulders in water, fishing late at night. His friends had managed to pull him free but it had been too late. I had thought it dumb. Now that the dry season was approaching, the floodwaters were receding fast and you could see up to twenty-seven crocs in a stretch of just three hundred metres of water. The day before yesterday I had seen a large crocodile floating like a dead log close behind a tiny newborn hippo that was following its mother through the water towards the shallows. With the afterbirth still flowing from her, the hippo must just have given birth, but thankfully she was able to move her baby closer to the raft. The incident had captured the endless cycle of life and death for me, the very essence of this wild, beautiful, savage place. But unlike the infant hippo, Boycat had not made it. Defeated and powerless over the loss of my little man's life, I sat down beside Poep, put my hands over my face and wept.

My mind raced back to the last time I had seen him, two days earlier. He had been in one of his typical bouncy moods, batting at my shoes and hoping to steal them from my hand but succeeding in slapping me on the eyelid instead. I'd counted myself lucky that for once he didn't have his claws out, otherwise I'd surely have lost my eye. Now it seemed a small price to pay if only he would just show up right now. I felt angry and cheated that I had not been able to see him one last time yesterday, the last day of his life, but I'd had to drive to Mfuwe to send a few faxes and some mail. On the way back I had stopped off for a bite of lunch at Tundwe Lodge and afterwards had gone slightly out of my way to drop someone off at their local village. By the time I got back to camp it was already fairly late in the afternoon.

Still I went out quickly to try to find them before nightfall, only to find both their tracks on the west bank going into the river. With the light fading, I had strung up some fresh meat for them in a tree before meeting Cha to enjoy the beautiful golden sunset as it descended over the river south of camp. I had felt certain Boycat and Poep would return to the island before dark and hoped they might still come round to visit the camp, not knowing that around that time …

Poepface turned her eyes back towards the water as if comprehending that this was the last place she had seen her brother, but she now allowed me to sit down quietly beside her. It almost killed me to see her like this and, desperate to try and distract her away from the place where she had seen Boycat die, I left after about an hour to fetch a chunk of meat from the camp fridge. She was gone when I returned. 'POEP!'I called again and again, 'POEP!' But if she was nearby she did not show herself.

Feeling utterly wretched, I went back to camp to look for Cha to tell her Boycat had been killed, without offering any elaboration. My throat was tight, I couldn't speak; couldn't say anything else. There was a stabbing pain in my chest as I tried to suppress my sobs, unable to share the depth of my grief with anyone, not even with her. She just nodded, her eyes full of sorrow, understanding I needed to be alone to deal with my emotions.

As I turned to go back to the west bank to look for Poep my eyes felt sore and my cheeks were wet and I was grateful that at least there was no one else around. Karin had left early to drive a very sick JV to the airport to catch a plane to Johannesburg where he would be admitted to hospital with a severe case of malaria. I was shivering as I made my way out of camp, understanding that I too was probably in the early stages of the disease. Gillian was already in hospital with malaria, having been flown out of the valley just days before. It was almost impossible not to contract malaria in the South Luangwa Valley.

Poep was back at the edge of the water and again I sat down next to her, grieving with her for her brother and for the spine-chilling distance I felt between us. She remained reserved and aloof and didn't want to be touched. I respected her sorrow and, not wishing to add to her anguish, I simply placed my hand beside her paw on the ground as a gesture of empathy and to try to evoke her usual reaction of lifting her foot and placing it on my hand and gently trying to lift it. But she just looked absent-mindedly at my hand without making any attempt to touch me.

We stayed together like this for six hours during which time she eventually and somewhat indifferently allowed me to bring up my hand to touch her face and neck and stroke her along the corner of her mouth and whiskers. After a while, she got up to seek shade and rest in a dense flame creeper thicket where I left her, not wanting to intrude. I got up wearily, deciding to take a look around and try to piece together the sequence of events the night before.

Maybe I'm wrong, I thought. *Maybe he's come out at a different section of the river*. A slight surge of hope began to stir as I began searching, combing every inch of the island and inspecting every possible place where he might have climbed up on to the river bank. But the sand only revealed the tracks of antelope. Coming back to the place where I had found Poep staring at the water I scrutinised the area where the cubs had left to swim towards the opposite mainland. Maybe he was still there? Hesitating only briefly, I took off my shoes. I peered intently at the surface of the water, looking for any sign of movement before wading into the river to emerge on dry land fifteen metres later. Finding both sets of their tracks I followed the footprints in the sand, discovering that the cubs had begun to run after a herd of puku. They had maintained the chase for about seventy metres across the sandbank before giving up and retracing their steps back to the shore to return to the island. Bending down and touching the tracks left behind by Boycat and Poep, I saw that they had entered the water only a few metres further south from where they had first come out. Casting my eyes over the stretch of water in front of me, I felt myself begin to choke. She had been the only one to reach the other bank.

Deadly. This river was deadly. I had known it before, but now I felt it and had the emotional scars to prove it. Almost indifferently I waded back in, not really caring about the treachery that might lurk deep below that ridiculously short fifteen metres of water or what might happen to me, except that I needed to be there for Poep. At its deepest level the water came halfway to my chest before the sandy river floor gradually rose beneath my feet and, climbing on to the bank, I went to look for Poep. No longer finding her beneath the thicket, I spent some time searching the area but when I failed to find her, I decided to leave her be for a while and set off back to camp.

I greeted Cha and then went straight to my tent feeling nauseous and cold, but just as I was about to open the flap I heard Cha calling out to me. 'Graham! Poep is there! Just behind you! She's followed you back!' Turning sharply, I hurried back to see Poepface emerge from the bush and, bending down beside her, I tried to reassure her. She allowed me to touch her but was still very tense. After speaking to her in a soothing voice, I quietly got up and fetched her some meat from the kitchen fridge, which thankfully she took. Sitting back down on the ground beside her as she finished her meal, I stroked her and stayed with her until the shadows began to lengthen. Then just before sunset she stood up and walked off into the bush along the game trail leading north of camp.

'Good night, my darling girl,' I whispered. 'Be careful out there.' I watched her disappear into the shadows wishing with all my heart that I could follow her.

As I lay in bed later that night, I felt beads of sweat trickling down the side of my face and my head felt as if it was going to explode. Restless and aching, and seeing Boycat in front of me, my weakened body was fast losing the battle with the malaria parasite. A diet of tinned food and the shock of losing Boycat were taking their toll, but I couldn't fail Poep and there was no way I'd leave her behind to go to hospital. Especially now that she was alone.

I dragged myself out of bed early the following morning and found my little girl at the edge of the western river bank again. This time when she heard my footsteps coming up behind her she turned her head and chuffed at me in greeting. *Thank God,* I thought. *There is still that intimacy between us.*

Together we sat by the water for a long time until she suddenly stood up and pricked her ears, focusing her attention intently on something in the bush. She looked expectant and excited and I felt my spirits rise knowing that if she thought she'd heard an animal rustling in the undergrowth she would have gone straight after it. Maybe ... Maybe Boycat had made it after all and was about to bound out of the thickets and ambush his sister and me ... The way she held her head and listened was exactly as she would before he pounced on her. I held my breath for several seconds but then she swivelled her ears one last time and dolefully turned back to stare silently at the water.

When Karin returned later that afternoon she refused to believe that Boycat was dead. Maintaining over the following days that he had merely made a successful transition into the wild, she concentrated on her film work, often spending time across the river with Elmon, Willie and Xingi at their camp. Since I had neither the energy nor the inclination to argue with her, I left Karin to think what she wanted. If only I'd found a shred of a clue, the faintest impression of a pug mark or a strand of hair I might have hoped that she was right. In my heart I knew he was gone, but I still kept looking. I searched every last inch of the island and beyond, on the park's mainland, south of camp on the sandbanks and even on the GMA, checking and rechecking every last possibility. Now that the Luangwa River no longer flowed in the north, dry, bright river sand was exposed where four weeks earlier Boycat and Poep had first crossed the water into the national park. If Boycat had reverted to a wild solitary existence, his footprints would have been clearly imprinted in the sand.

On the morning of 10 May 1994, after I'd spent hours searching for any sign of her brother, I found Poep sitting next to a small stand of *Peltophorum africanum* trees on the west bank, close to where she thought she had heard her brother the day before. Her fur shone in the early morning light and she looked up at me as I approached.

'Hello, my darling girl,' I said, sitting down next to her. I was feeling exhausted, fragile and increasingly ill. Looking up, I saw a troop of baboons wanting to cross the river from the opposite bank, close to where Boycat and Poep had entered the water together for the last time. *Don't*, I wanted to warn them, you have no idea how dangerous that water is. Almost too afraid to look, I watched them braving the river and was relieved to see every last one of them make it safely across to the island shore.

When I returned to camp several hours later I saw Cha, Karin and John huddled around the radio in the kitchen tent. They were listening intently to a man's voice crackling over the static and didn't notice me.

'This is the BBC,' the broadcaster announced. 'Nelson Mandela has become South Africa's first black president after more than three centuries of white rule. Mr Mandela's African National Congress party won 252 of the 400 seats in the first democratic elections in South Africa's history. The inauguration ceremony took place in the Union Buildings amphitheatre in Pretoria today, attended by politicians and dignitaries from more than one hundred and forty countries around the world ...'

I knew it was a momentous day for my country but I couldn't bring myself to join the others to listen any further. I just wanted to be alone. But as I walked towards my tent, I heard our new president address his nation.

'*Wat is verby is verby* ...' Nelson Mandela's words rang in my ears. The past is the past. It was true. Boycat had gone. My beautiful, gorgeous boy was now no more than a treasured memory.

TWO LARGE LIONESSES were sauntering lazily across the dry sand on to the northern bank of the island. Moving slowly through the tall grass, they walked past an area of winter thorn trees and *Grewia* bushes and across a flat open area until they once again felt grass beneath their feet. As they headed south one of the lionesses stopped to smell the air. Raising her chin towards the scent, her sister also detected the alluring smell of fresh meat. Inquisitively, the lionesses stood together sniffing the air before turning sharply west. Purposefully starting to walk faster, the females soon broke into a trot, intent on quickly closing the distance between themselves and the small leopard feeding on fresh meat.

I FELT SOMEWHAT better when I woke shortly before dawn the following day. The Halfan antimalarial tablets Karin had brought back from town had finally kicked in and relieved me off the feverish sweats and dreadful headaches. Once again the air felt cool and crisp and, stepping into the early morning, I set off along a well-worn game path back to the thicket where I'd left a fresh impala carcass for Poep the previous evening. Then, stopping abruptly, I noticed the tracks of two large lionesses heading straight for the thicket. They were fresh. Very fresh. Perhaps an hour old; maybe even less.

My heart began to pound as I checked the immediate area carefully and, interpreting the tracks, I saw from the scuffmarks that the two females had started running, parting ways to rush in towards their prey in a classic pincer movement. I couldn't allow myself even to contemplate what might have happened so I concentrated on one set of tracks before checking the other. When I did not find a dead leopard at the end of either set I felt hugely relieved and began to search for Poep's footprints. I came across them a little further on, heading towards a young sausage tree about twenty metres ahead of me. Breaking into a run, I hurried towards the tree and, catching a glimpse of her golden and black coat, I saw her safely tucked in a fork in the tree trunk.

'POEP!' I called, before giving two short puffs. 'Are you all right?' She responded to my chuffing but, clearly confused and scared, she refused to move or come down out of the tree.

I should have hoisted that meat for her, I thought. *How could I have been so stupid? God knows how it might have ended.* I stayed with her for over an hour, standing at the base of the sausage tree and talking to her but failing to persuade her to come down. Her eyes, like Boycat's when he had come into camp, had taken on a completely different expression. There was something unfathomable in those beautiful green eyes: the loss of her beloved brother, her brush with the lionesses and a heightened awareness of the dangers in her new world.

The following morning I followed her tracks into the long grass on the north-west bank and found her resting close to some thickets. I had brought meat with me and she responded excitedly, appearing a lot more confident and in better spirits, although she wasn't keen to be touched. It pained me but I respected her wishes.

Early the next day I found her back on the west bank, still a little tense and not wanting to be fussed over, and still checking the water for her brother. Her eyes seemed to reflect a resistance to what she had been forced to accept; the certainty that he was never coming back again. My heart went out to her. I knew exactly how she was feeling.

During the next three days I found Poep in different areas, west of the winter thorn thicket, lying under a bush on the north bank, and slinking through a thicket not far from camp to stalk a pronking puku. Good, I thought, she is hunting bigger stuff now. When she came to greet me she seemed a little brighter and less sad, which made me feel more confident for her.

The following morning marked ten days that Boycat had been gone. It was May 17. Leaving camp shortly after dawn, I checked in all the usual places without finding any sign of Poep. Growing increasingly concerned, I finally saw her on the south bank of the island trying to cross the river at a point where there was a series of small sandbanks. Calling her, I watched her as she looked up and emerged from a shallow pool of water looking terrified. Any hope I might have had for Boycat were dashed in that moment. We sat on the dry bank together and as I stroked her head and brushed my fingers along the edge of her mouth and whiskers, I was grateful that we still shared something special. After a while Poep followed me back to camp. I fetched some meat for her and left her to drag it off behind the storage tent to feed in peace.

When I went back to check on her just before sunset she had gone.

'Don't try to cross that river, little girl,' I whispered. 'Be safe tonight.'

As I joined Cha, Karin and John for supper by the fire, I wondered which direction I should take the next morning when I went to look for her. I did not know that I would never see her again.

18

SEND THE WIND OVER MY FOOTPRINTS

The South Luangwa Valley
13 June 1994

There was a rustle outside, followed by the short snap of a twig close to my head on the other side of the tent canvas. It woke me instantly as any tiny sound had done since the cubs started staying out at night. I listened intently. Something was definitely outside, padding softly on the crisp discarded leaves of the Natal mahogany that towered over the roof of the tent. The footfalls were too light to be a hyena and it couldn't be a lion because I would have heard its characteristic heavy breathing. No, it was something else. I strained my ears for a clue, trying to ignore the hammering in my head and the cold shivers that the Halfan medication could no longer suppress. Was it real? Or just a cruel figment of my imagination – a feverish dream?

I closed my eyes until I heard the sound again. *There!* I instantly sat up in bed. It was Poep; I had never been so sure of anything in my life before. Shivering with fever, I swung my legs over the edge of the bed and fumbled for matches on the bedside table, managing to retrieve one from the box and, with slightly trembling fingers, to sweep the tip along the striking surface.

Holding the wavering flame across the blackened wick of the paraffin lamp, I watched as a soft halo of light gradually illuminated our possessions like new-found treasures in a mummy's tomb. I felt the dampness of the sheet beneath my palms as, using my hands to support myself, I stood up on unsteady legs.

Stumbling towards the cupboard to find a pair of shorts, I reached for the torch, hoping it still had enough power for me to shine into the darkness outside, but after flicking the switch a few times I realised its batteries were exhausted. I cursed silently and slapped the handle hard against my thigh until a feeble beam of powdery light forced itself from the torch head. Shuffling back to the bed, I bent down to raise the glass of the paraffin lamp to extinguish the sputtering flame when Cha began to stir.

'Graham?' She sat up in bed and looked at me questioningly, her short fair hair tousled from sleep.

'Shhhhhh!' I said. 'Poep is outside. I have to go and see her. Go back to sleep.' Without waiting for her to reply I blew out the flame and turned to reach down for the zipper in the tent flap, pulling it halfway up and reeling at the screeching sound it made.

Twenty-seven days. It'd been almost a month since she had disappeared from camp that afternoon I had seen her trying to cross the river at the sandbanks. When I followed her tracks leading away from camp early the next morning, I found that Poep had headed north along a game trail where her footprints disappeared on the hard ground. I picked up her spoor again on the bank of the now dry river, crossing the thick sand to the park mainland only a very short distance from where she and Boycat had first left the island a month earlier when the Luangwa was still flowing. I followed them on the other bank but lost them again on the band of small stones and pebbles stretching along the higher flood line. I looked everywhere, searching for even the faintest of clues but finding only a few scattered sand particles on the rocks where they had brushed off the pads of her feet. She simply disappeared, eleven days after Boycat had gone missing.

I went out every day from then onwards, searching for her, searching for him – just in case the cubs had somehow met up again and were lying low in the bush waiting to ambush me. I checked every last gully, the smallest dongas and all the places she loved; the groves, the flame creepers, the area west of the winter thorn thicket, the west bank, the north bank and every little bush in between without finding a single trace.

Every morning and every afternoon I set out, feeling increasingly despairing as I found not a shred of evidence of either Boycat or Poep. I was frail, weakened by malaria, but at the same time it became my shield, for no one could tell that while I was madly shivering I was really just sobbing my heart out.

About ten days after she vanished I heard Sam screaming blue murder very early in the morning. I'd had a particularly bad night with severe fever and excruciating headaches and was still in bed but, heaving myself up off the soaked sheets, I left the tent to see him standing by the kitchen pointing to the bush. Recalling the last time the cubs had come into camp just before dawn and had scared Sam's replacement, I felt slightly hopeful as I asked him what he had seen. When he told me that a large leopard had slunk along a thicket just minutes earlier but had run off at the sound of his raised voice my optimism was dashed. I didn't believe either Poep or Boycat would have been intimidated by Sam or anyone else in camp, even though from the day they arrived in Zambia I had kept them away from people as much as possible, interacting with them only when I knew Sam and John were resting in their tents or away from camp. Still, I couldn't pass up any opportunity. I knew I was grasping at straws but I quickly checked the area only to find the tracks of a much older leopard.

That had been seventeen days ago. Now, in the deep pre-dawn darkness with only a feeble beam of light that barely penetrated the bush I was once again hopeful. Left, right, left, right, I shone the torch around the bush in a wide semicircular movement, but couldn't see anything. Feeling another feverish shiver run along my spine, I wondered for a moment whether I had just imagined her footsteps. Why would she come back now, just days before we were to fly back to South Africa? I stopped, listening hard when I heard another sound. *There! Again!* She was really here, about fifteen metres ahead of me but she was now moving slowly away from camp. I chuffed at her. *Pfff pfff.* The footsteps stopped, pausing for a few seconds as if she was undecided about what to do. Then she carried on walking.

'Noooooo!' Sounding shrill and weak, I barely recognised my own voice as it rang over the bush. *'Don't go! Pooeeeep! Please don't go!'*

I desperately wanted to follow her, but it was too dark, too dangerous. All I could do was look for her tracks outside the wall of the tent. Shining the feeble light in front of me, I found a mosaic of footprints clearly visible in the soft sand; they were hers. Poep had been lingering directly in line with my head on the opposite side of the canvas. Then after a while she had gradually and determinedly begun moving back into the night.

My heart leapt and I almost burst with joy. My little girl had made it; she was fine and living wild. I'd never doubted her ability to survive, knowing she was smart and more than able to take care of herself, but I still worried for her.

Frustrated by the darkness, I cursed the danger that kept me from going after her, robbing me of the chance to spend a last time with her. *I had to see her.* If it were up to me I'd stay there for ever because even if I no longer saw Poep at least I'd be close to wherever she was. But Cha and I were booked on the first available flight to South Africa where I had to be admitted to hospital or risk losing my life. In a few days the camp would be dismantled and Karin and John would be moving to Xingi's camp. It was part of the agreement I had made with JV; that once the cubs had disappeared for more than a month we would leave because this would mean they were either surviving as wild leopards, or they were dead.

Dithering outside the tent until a grey mantle of pre-dawn light finally began to descend over the bush and with just enough light to make out rough shapes I bolted down the narrow game trail armed only with the dim torchlight to guide me.

'Pooooeeeep! Wait! Wait for me!' I hurried past the cubs' cage heading straight towards the north bank, past the Natal mahogany out of which Boycat had pulled me and his food a lifetime ago.

Brushing its pale light over the early morning, the sun pushed its orange head over the horizon. Now that I could see more clearly I dropped the torch and began to run. Spiky thickets with hungry, greedy thorns caught at the skin on my bare legs, lacerating my calves, but I didn't feel anything and just kept going, running all the way to the north bank where I eventually stopped beside her fresh footprints in the soft river sand. The landscape before me was shrouded in pink light and I narrowed my eyes and swept them over the valley floor, watching for the slightest of movements and hoping for at least a final glimpse. She'd have learnt by now that she was vulnerable in the open, I thought. Remaining covert and using the bush to camouflage her golden rosetted fur was key to survival. It was her new way. It was the leopard's way.

Concentrating on the tracks, I followed where she had gone, moving further east alongside the dry riverbed before she had begun to cross. Tumbling down the bank, I sprinted across the wide expanse of sand, flying over her tracks and up the other side. On I ran, past the area of high grass where the lioness had stalked Cha and me when we sitting on the bank a few days after Boycat and Poep had crossed the river.

'Poeeeeeeep!' I called again and again. *'Poeeeeep! Wait for me!'* To my left I saw the deep gully that ran like an artery into the national park, but instead of moving deeper into the bush over the sand she had padded towards a sea of chest-high grass and that was where I lost her tracks. Slowing my pace, I parted the green shoots randomly, frantically searching for a sense of direction. Swishing left and right, deeper into the vegetation, I found only rough, three-pointed old hippo tracks that had long since been baked hard by the sun. Going forward cautiously I stared at the mass of indentations in the solidified clay. The soft padded feet of a leopard would not leave any impressions there and I knew that it would be futile to try to follow her any further.

Raising my eyes to look over the tall grass I saw the thick mopane forest looming like a skyscraper on the edge of the virtually impenetrable ten thousand square kilometres of untamed wilderness. At that moment I became aware of an almost eerie silence. I couldn't hear anything. Not a single bird call, no buzz of a fly, no sound of a small animal scurrying through the undergrowth. Where had the insects gone? None of it made sense. It was as if the entire South Luangwa Valley was holding its breath, like an orchestra waiting for the conductor to lift his baton in anticipation of the grand finale. I felt strangely suspended in time and my mind grappled with the physical world around me before I finally came to grips with what had happened. My little Poepface didn't want me to follow her. She didn't want to be found. She had come to say goodbye.

'No!' The last of my strength gave way and I felt my knees collapsing beneath me as I sank to the ground like a man who had been shot in the back.

The baton came down and the score ended. Everything around me seemed to fade as I held my hands to my eyes and wept, cradled only by the compassionate arms of silence. She was following the beat of a different drum now and I could no longer hold on. My heart ached as the seconds ticked by and she strode ever deeper into the wilderness, creating a distance between us that would never be bridged again.

Poepface had gone home.

EPILOGUE

With an ear-splitting noise the Boeing 737 revved its engines and, lurching forward, the plane picked up speed as it thundered along the tarmac before lifting off into the clear blue sky.

Resting my forehead wearily against the small window I looked down with clouded eyes, searching the rapidly shrinking landscape below us and hoping for a final glimpse of the island. Mfuwe airport quickly disappeared from view and a vast wilderness of dark green bush stretched out lethargically beneath me. In the distance I caught sight of the Luangwa River, sparkling in the late morning sunlight, twisting and turning along the valley floor like a giant water serpent. Somewhere there, I thought. She was somewhere down there by herself. A knife-like pain flashed through my heart. I had left her there alone. Tears began to choke me again; I was surprised I had any left to spill. I felt as if I were in a dream, a horrible, painful nightmare. My eyes hurt and my cheeks were wet as I stared at the stubble of green, wondering where she was and what she was doing. It wasn't long before midday; pcrhaps she had climbed high into a Natal mahogany tree, shielding her dappled body from the searing heat. Beside me, I felt Cha give my arm a reassuring squeeze, but I did not turn to her; I had to keep my eyes locked on the South Luangwa Valley for as long as I could.

It had been six days since Poep had come to my tent and everything that had happened after that was more or less a blur. I remembered lying flat on my stomach close to where she had slipped between the grasses to disappear for ever, wanting to scream and be swallowed up by the sand. My little Poepface had come to me, but I had not been able to say goodbye properly; it was something I knew I would never come to accept, cope with or lay to rest.

I have no idea how long I stayed there afterwards. Eventually I sat up, my eyes no longer wet, but my cheeks covered in mud where the soft river sand had caked my tears. I was an emotional and physical wreck. Both from losing her and from the malaria. The fevers and uncontrollable sweats had consumed me even after I'd taken the last of the six Halfan tablets two days earlier and the parasite had returned with a vengeance, crippling my already weakened body.

I hated myself for getting malaria and hated having to leave the island, but I knew I had to be hospitalised. Any recollection of walking back to camp evaded my mind, but I remember that it was scorching hot by the time I got there. What happened in the days after that was beyond me. I was too sick to be conscious of anything other than that she had gone, but we couldn't leave because all the airlines were fully booked and the first available seats to Johannesburg via Lusaka were that morning, 19 June.

Carrying just two duffel bags Karin, Cha and I left the island and walked across the floodplain towards the dinghy, passing the small series of sandbanks where Poep had tried to cross the river before following me back to camp only a few weeks earlier. I tried not to think and just to concentrate on walking, but I dreaded every step that took me further from the island and from her. The hurt grew stronger as I mechanically placed one foot in front of the other and all I really wanted was to turn around and run back to stay there for ever, but I couldn't allow myself to succumb to that urge because it would have killed me. I had to try to find a way to handle this, knowing what the cubs and I had shared would be the most beautiful and the most painful thing in my entire life.

After rowing across the Luangwa River to the GMA, I insisted that Karin and Cha sit in the front seat beside me while I got behind the wheel for the trip to Mfuwe. I was probably too sick to drive, but I needed to hold on to the steering wheel so that my splitting head could deal with the bumps along the rutted road. After a long, hot, bone-jarring drive, we reached the small airport of Mfuwe. Karin came with us into the terminal building as we made our way to the check-in counter and received our boarding passes. We didn't really talk much. I think Karin and I both realised what an incredible experience we'd had with the cubs and there was really nothing more to say about it. I'd been hard on her at times, but that was because I worried about the cubs' safety as well as hers. It no longer mattered; that was all behind us now. She hugged Cha and me goodbye before turning to make the long drive back.

After changing planes in Lusaka Cha and I finally emerged into the arrivals hall at Jan Smuts International Airport where three familiar faces stood out from a hazy crowd of patiently waiting people. There was Celia, my sister, and Cha's parents, Jimmy and Sally Supra.

Celia's eyes were dark with consternation and shock when she saw me leaning heavily on a luggage trolley for support as we moved towards them through the hubbub of people. She had known on the last evening of her visit to Londolozi before we left for Zambia that parting from Boycat and Poepface would mark me for life. But now, instead of facing the fairly strong, healthy man she had kissed goodbye, she saw a hollow-eyed, cadaverous person whose skin was yellow and whose body was much too thin.

Wasting no time on niceties, Celia immediately bundled me into her white VW Beetle and tore on to the highway where the hectic afternoon traffic kept her on the edge of her seat all the way to the Brenthurst Clinic in

Hillbrow which we reached more than an hour later. Even there everything got bogged down by bureaucracy. Mad as a snake at the nurses who wanted me to complete a stack of forms before admitting me, Celia made a huge fuss until the nurses were eventually persuaded to page a doctor to admit me while she completed the admin.

'I know my brother better than anybody,' she spat. 'And if you don't treat him immediately he is going to die!' This was instantly effective and Dr Pinkus, a malaria specialist who had also treated Gillian and JV a few weeks earlier, arrived shortly afterwards.

Being cooped up in a hospital bed with a bunch of strange people was the last thing I thought I could cope with and, afraid I would go mad in the sterile environment, I tried to persuade the doctor to treat me as an out-patient. But Dr Pinkus told Celia I was severely ill and needed to be put on a drip straight away.

I ended up staying in a one-bed ward for ten days before eventually being discharged to face some very grim demons. Boycat was dead. And my darling Poepface had become part of a world in which I had no place. Her face kept flashing in front of me and I yearned to know if she was okay. Was she still mourning for her brother? Did she think of me sometimes?

The other thing was that I was out of a job. Londolozi had recently been taken over by a new corporate management team and I was no longer on the payroll. Instead, I was back in the big concrete jungle where hooting cars and glaring lights replaced the soothing snorts of hippos wallowing in the river and the prattling and chirping of small birds against the backdrop of a softly rustling breeze. Every night I fell into bed exhausted, yet sleepless, spilling more hot tears into the pillow. Crying for the loss of him. Crying for the loss of her. There wasn't a day, an hour, a minute that I didn't think of them and in the many years that have passed the void they left behind has not diminished. In time, this became its own comfort. The pain that was left behind became a trusted friend; the only tangible reminder of what I had shared with them.

About ten days after I left the hospital my father and I travelled to Londolozi to fetch my car and last few personal items that had been kept in storage for me. My heart began to beat a little faster as we entered the reserve to the south-west, driving north along the fence line before reaching the old railway line and coming out in open grass and mixed woodland before arriving at the airstrip. Only three months earlier Boycat and Poep had been here, taking off in an airplane to Zambia where I had been eagerly awaiting them. I tried not to think, concentrating on the drive until we were over the dam wall and had pulled into the staff car park when I quickly nipped into the garage to collect the keys of my old Jetta from Ray and to gather my belongings. I did not linger. Even if I had wanted to, I couldn't go back to where my old camp had stood on the banks of the Inyatini riverbed; it hurt too much.

That night, lying in bed and listening to the noise of the city roads, I thought of the Dudley Males and imagined the brothers standing together in the moonless night, their deep voices bellowing over the bush proclaiming their ownership of the territory south of the dry Xabene riverbed. I would never know what fate befell the two brothers, or that of the Castleton Females and their eight large cubs, nor any of the other lions and leopards I had come to know so well for I never again returned to Londolozi. Today they have all gone, including Xingi, who was savagely attacked by five large lionesses and died of her injuries a short time after Cha and I left the South Luangwa Valley.

After spending ten months at Phinda Forest Lodge, I founded and ran Eco-Training with my old pal Jimmy Marshall and Wayne Mclintock. This was conceptualised as both a practical and theoretical training course for potential young field guides. A year later, Cha and I returned to Zambia to work for Puku Pan Safari Lodge on the banks of the Kafue River, about three hundred kilometres south-west of the island, before we returned to South Africa where we got married in August 1996.

Boycat and Poep have affected my entire life. I realised I was never an easy person to get to know, but they allowed me to accept myself and my idiosyncrasies. By being with them and observing their behaviour they taught me to analyse situations before diving into them and to be cautious about those with whom I associated. This made me a tougher person emotionally because I knew that nothing would ever again be as traumatic for me as losing them. When I stood up to speak at my father's funeral service in January 2011 I was acutely aware that I had experienced the same level of grief before – and had in fact gone beyond it. And even then, they were there with me. There are things I remember daily, and sometimes I have to laugh at myself because I instinctively size people up to determine whether their intentions are in any way devious. For the most part this has served me well when forming first impressions of those I meet. Boycat in particular taught me about the advantages of wearing a blank expression so that people cannot read your eyes. He excelled at reading people's minds and it was only because I learnt to observe his behaviour so assiduously that I didn't get ripped up more often.

I would not have hesitated to give my life for my leopards and I doubt that even my closest friends can truly understand the depth of our relationship. We may have had only a short time together, but for me it will never truly end.

A few years ago, in August 2009, I heard the news that an old leopard had died at Londolozi. She was known to the rangers as the 3:4 female, but I remembered her best as the little Tugwaan girl who had given Boycat his first bash in the bush and had watched me covertly from behind the scented thorn tree, intrigued to hear a human speak her language. She was seventeen years old.

I thought of my little Poepface and her wary nature that would have served her so well and hoped that she too had made it to an advanced age. Closing my eyes, I imagined her still alive, padding silently in the shadows of the South Luangwa Valley.

ACKNOWLEDGEMENTS

As with any major project there have been a number of people whose support, input, enthusiasm and backing have been invaluable.

GRAHAM

For Charmian

You holy Art, when all my hope is shaken,
And through life's raging tempest I am drawn,
You make my heart with warmest love to waken,
As if into a better world reborn.

An Die Musik, translated by Basil Swift

Nick Marx for his friendship and for sharing his knowledge and the depth of his passion with me and for all the advice he gave me regarding the cubs. Fransje, for all you have done with the book and what you have been through to get it on paper. Paul Gibbons, Melly Lawson, Pete and Yvonne Short, Jimmy Marshall, Trevor Brown, Justine Fouchi, Paul Buck and the production crew for making the filming a memorable time in my life. Karin and Andries for their assistance with the cubs and the good times we had. My sister Celia for listening to me and for understanding. Mark Tennant for the years of friendship and use of his photographs. Jan Rombouts for pushing me to get it turned into a book, Shirley Phelan for her endless support and Carlson Mathebula and all the other trackers and staff I became friends with at Londolozi. Too many to name individually, but you all know who you are, Trev Lindegger, Rich de la Rey, Al Rankin, Lyn and Lex Hes, Tony and Dee Adams, BJ Watson, Jane Crossley, Rich Siwela, Patson, Johnston, to name but some of them, and John Varty for giving me the opportunity of a lifetime. Carlson, in particular, I thank you for teaching me how to understand and interpret the wild and those who live there and for taking the time to open your eyes and your heart to me. My mom and dad for instilling a passion for anything natural in me. Poep and Boy for allowing me to be their friend, companion and guardian and for returning my affection with compound interest. All the people I met and spent time with in Zambia, and Brooke Shields for the humility she showed when working with my babies and me.

FRANSJE

Thank you, Graham, for sharing your incredible story with me and for making me feel as though I knew Boycat and Poep as surely as if I had spent time with them. My thanks to Alison Lowry and Renei Naudı at Penguin Books in Johannesburg for their enthusiasm and to my editor Pam Thornley whose patience, hard work and insights are much appreciated. A massive thank you to Celia Ruinard: your feedback, ideas and suggestions came at a time when I most needed them; to Lex Hes for his assistance and information on the leopards of Londolozi; Nick Marx for his thoughts and insights about the cubs; Melly Lawson – thank you so much for your time and for sharing your views; Paul Gibbons for the coffees, conversations and photos and for allowing me to pick his brain; Adam Twidell, Jim Brockett, Therese Haigh and Saul Basley for their help and information on the aviation industry; to Mark Tennant for his emotive photographs of Graham and the cubs, and to Charmian Cooke for being quietly supportive in the background during the many months I kept her husband glued to his email. To my family, Jan, Toja, Daisy and Anne van Riel for their support; Hedy de Bats for her enthusiasm and the creation of my beautiful website; Frank Meijer for checking in with me on Skype every day while I was writing; Debbie Hollen for just being there; Corine Snel for incredible kindness; and, in Sydney, a very special thank you to Romany Sloan for her tireless support and love. To Smudge, Mommy and Boytjie for their inspiration and companionship during the 500-odd days I was cooped up indoors writing. And lastly, to Boycat and Poepface – I feel privileged to have known you.